Edward Y. Odisho

The Sound System of Modern Assyrian

(Neo-Aramaic)

Semitica Viva · Band 2

Herausgegeben von Otto Jastrow

Edward Y. Odisho

The Sound System of Modern Assyrian (Neo-Aramaic)

1988

Otto Harrassowitz · Wiesbaden

Edward Y. Odisho

The Sound System of Modern Assyrian (Neo-Aramaic)

1988

Otto Harrassowitz · Wiesbaden

SEMITICA VIVA

CIP-Titelaufnahme der Deutschen Bibliothek

Odisho, Edward:
The sound system of modern Assyrian (Neo-Aramaic) / Edward Odisho. - Wiesbaden : Harrassowitz, 1988
  (Semitica viva ; Bd. 2)
ISBN 978-3-447-02744-1
NE: GT

Sigel: SV

© Otto Harrassowitz, Wiesbaden 1988. Alle Rechte vorbehalten.
Otto Harrassowitz GmbH & Co. KG Kreuzberger Ring 7c-d, D-65205 Wiesbaden,
produktsicherheit.verlag@harrassowitz.de
Photographische und photomechanische Wiedergabe
nur mit ausdrücklicher Genehmigung des Verlages.
Printed with grants from the Assyrian Academic Society and the David Perley Fund.
Satz: Satz-Offizin Hümmer GmbH, 8702 Waldbüttelbrunn
Printed in Germany.

TO

THE LATE DR. DAVID PERLEY

A SYMBOL OF KNOWLEDGE AND DEVOTION

TABLE OF CONTENTS

LIST OF ILLUSTRATIONS XI

TRANSCRIPTION CONVENTIONS AND SYMBOLS XIII
ACKNOWLEDGEMENTS.. XVII
INTRODUCTION 1

I. AN ETHNOLINGUISTIC HISTORY OF ASSYRIANS 3

    1.1. The Neo-Aramaic Language.................................. 3
    1.2. Aramaic Language But Assyrian Descent 5
    1.3. Concluding Remarks....................................... 16

II. STANDARD WRITTEN NEO-ARAMAIC LANGUAGE AND SPOKEN KOINE 19

    2.1. Introductory Remarks...................................... 19
    2.2. The Emergence of Standard Written NA Language........... 19
    2.3. Further Development and Spread of the Koine............. 21
    2.4. Further Demographic and Social Changes and the
         Consolidation of the Koine 23
    2.5. Some Salient Phonetic and Phonological Similarities and
         Differences Between the Koine and the Urmi Dialect 24
    2.6. Inconsistencies Within the Koine 27

III. THE CONSONANTAL SYSTEM.. 39

    3.1. Introductory Remarks...................................... 39
    3.2. Theoretical Approaches and Practical Criteria of Investigation 39
    3.3. Controversial Sounds and Alphabetic Representation 43
    3.4. Inventory of the Koine Consonants 44
    3.5. Conventions for the Interpretation of the Chart 44

IV. THE VOWEL SYSTEM... 51

    4.1. Introductory Remarks...................................... 51
    4.2. Methods of Investigation 51

	4.3. Syllable Structures and Patterns in Polysyllabic Words	52
	4.4. Syllable Structures and Patterns in Monosyllabic Words	54
	4.5. Some Less Common Syllable Structures and Patterns	55
	4.6. Further Distributional Examination and Concluding Remarks	56
	4.7. Some Salient Characteristics of the Vowel System	57
	4.8. Similar Trends of Change in the Koine and in Urmi	58
V.	CONSONANT CLUSTERS	62
	5.1. Introductory Remarks	62
	5.2. Size of Clusters	63
	5.3. Structural Location of Clusters	63
	5.4. Types of Clusters	64
	5.5. Concluding Remarks	64
	5.6. Lists of Stems Containing the Attested Unemphatic Clusters	67
	5.7. Lists of Stems Containing the Attested Emphatic Clusters	73
VI.	STRESS AND INTONATION	79
	6.1. Introductory Remarks	79
	6.2. Stress and Rhythm	79
	6.3. Stress and Rhythm in the Koine	81
	6.4. Word Stress and Stem Stress	83
	6.5. Stress in Longer Pieces	85
	6.6. Rhythm in the Koine	87
	6.7. Pitch Patterns: Tones and Intonations	88
	6.8. Pitch Patterns in the Koine	89
VII.	METHODS AND INSTRUMENTATION	94
	7.1. Material and General Experimental Procedures	94
	7.2. Major Experiments	94
VIII.	ARTICULATORY, AERODYNAMIC AND ACOUSTIC DESCRIPTION OF CONSONANTS	98
	8.1. Introductory Remarks	98
	8.2. Plosive Production	98
	8.3. Bilabial Plosives	99
	8.4. Alveolar Plosives	101
	8.5. Palatal Plosives	102
	8.6. Voiceless (Unaspirated) Uvular Plosive	103

	8.7. Glottal Plosive (Stop)	104
	8.8. Palato-Alveolar Affricates	105
	8.9. Alveolar Fricatives	107
	8.10. Palato-Alveolar Fricatives	108
	8.11. Uvular Fricatives	109
	8.12. Voiceless Glottal Fricative	110
	8.13. Central Approximants	111
	8.14. Lateral Approximant	112
	8.15. Nasal Approximants	112
	8.16. Alveolar Tap	113

IX. A PHONETIC DESCRIPTION OF EMPHASIS 114

    9.1. Introductory Remarks 114
    9.2. Consonants in Emphatic Contexts 115
    9.3. Vowels in Emphatic Contexts 117
    9.4. Concluding Remarks 119

X. A PHONETIC DESCRIPTION OF DOUBLE PLOSIVE CLUSTERS 120

    10.1. Introductory Remarks 120
    10.2. Double-Plosive Clusters 121
    10.3. Discussion and Conclusion 123

APPENDIX 127

BIBLIOGRAPHY 143

LIST OF ILLUSTRATIONS

Figure

1. Consonantal Inventory of the Koine 45
2. Schematic Representation of the Manner of Articulation of Consonants 47
3. An Impressionistic Plotting of Vowels in the Koine 57
4. Vowel Diagram Showing the Contraction of the Diphthongs /ay/ and /aɥ(w)/ into the Monophthongs /e/ and /o/, respectively 59
5. Vowel Diagram Showing the Shift of /e/, /o/ Vowels into /i/, /u/, Respectively 60
6. Vowel Diagram Combining the Vocalic Shifts in Figs. 4 and 5 and Indicating the Systematicness of the Shift 61
7. Chart Showing the Attested Unemphatic Stem-Clusters in the Koine 65
8. Chart Showing the Attested Emphatic Stem-Clusters in the Koine ... 66
9. A Schematic Representation of the Types of Glottograms 97
10. a, b, c, d, e, f Pressure Patterns for /bd/, /ɟd/, /pt/, /pc/, /p^ht^h/ and /t^hp^h/ 122
11. Traces Based on Real Tokens of (a) Glottograms (Up), (b) Intraoral Pressure Pulses (Down) for /p/, /p^h/, and /b/ in the Contexts of /pida/, /p^hida/ and /bina/ 128
12. Traces Based on Real Tokens of (a) Glottograms (Up), (b) Intraoral Pressure Pulses (Down) for /č/ and /$č^h$/ in the Contexts of /čurˈčɪrrɪ/ and /$č^h$ɪrˈ$č^h$ɪrrɪ/ 129
13. Traces Based on Real Tokens of (a) Glottograms (Up), (b) Intraoral Pressure Pulses (Down) for the Clusters /bd/, /ɟd/, /p^ht^h/ and /t^hp^h/ in the Contexts of /bdaya/, /ɟdala/, /p^ht^haya/ and /t^hp^hana/ 130
14. Spectrograms 1–19 131

TRANSCRIPTION CONVENTIONS AND SYMBOLS

An attempt has been made to abide by the International Phonetic Alphabet (IPA); however, a few changes were inevitable. The limited digression from IPA was motivated by two reasons: (1) Render the transcription relatively consistent with the transcriptions available in the literature on NA. (2) Simplify the graphic rendition of some of the unfamiliar sounds that recur in this particular dialect of NA.

In the articulatory description of vowel height, the classificatory terms of *close, half-close, half-open,* and *open* are preferred to *high, mid* and *low* because of the belief that the former category provides better distinction and less confusion, especially inasmuch as the so-called mid-vowels are concerned.

SYMBOL   PHONETIC DESCRIPTION

i	front, close, with spread lips
ɪ	front (somewhat centralized), close to half-close, with spread lips
e	front, half-close to half-open, with spread lips
a	front, half-open to open, with unrounded (neutral) lips
ɑ	back, open, with unrounded (neutral) lips (typical emphatic vowel)
o	back, half-close to half-open, with rounded lips
u	back, close, with rounded lips
ü	front, close with rounded lips
ə	schwa
~	superimposed on a vowel indicates emphasis
b	voiced bilabial plosive
p	voiceless unaspirated bilabial plosive
p^h	voiceless aspirated bilabial plosive
d	voiced alveolar plosive
t	voiceless unaspirated alveolar plosive
t^h	voiceless aspirated alveolar plosive
ɟ	voiced palatal plosive
c	voiceless unaspirated palatal plosive
c^h	voiceless aspirated palatal plosive
g	voiced velar plosive
k	voiceless unaspirated velar plosive

XIV   Transcription Conventions and Symbols

kʰ	voiceless aspirated velar plosive
q	voiceless unaspirated uvular plosive
ʔ	glottal stop (plosive)
ṭs	voiceless unaspirated alveolar affricate (emphatic)
ǰ	voiced palato-alveolar affricate
č	voiceless unaspirated palato-alveolar affricate
čʰ	voiceless aspirated palato-alveolar affricate
ð	voiced inter-dental fricative
θ	voiceless inter-dental fricative
z	voiced alveolar fricative
s	voiceless alveolar fricative
ž	voiced palato-alveolar fricative
š	voiceless palato-alveolar fricative
ġ	voiced uvular fricative
x	voiceless uvular fricative
ʕ	voiced pharyngeal fricative
h	voiceless glottal (laryngeal) fricative
r	voiced alveolar tap = [ɾ]
l	lateral alveolar approximant[1]
y	central palatal approximant
ɥ	central labio-palatal approximant
w	central labio-velar approximant
m	nasal bilabial approximant
n	nasal alveolar approximant
:	length in vowels
·	half-length in vowels
/ /	phonemic transcription
[ ]	phonetic transcription
+	placed outside / / or [ ] indicates an abbreviated representation of emphasis

A detailed phonetic representation of emphasis is indicated in the following manner:

a) A dot under the following consonants

[b p pʰ d t tʰ ɟ c cʰ q ʔ ǰ čʰ z s ž š ġ x h r l y m n]

---

[1] All approximants are voiced, so "voicing" sounds redundant here.

Transcription Conventions and Symbols

b) Due to a major change in the place of articulation, emphasis in the following two consonants is indicated as follows:

[č] as [tṣ] and [ɥ] as [w]

c) A tilde placed above the following vowels:

i ɪ e o u

d) Because [ɑ] represents the typical features of emphasis and is a common symbol, it is used to stand for the emphatic counterpart of [a]

In an attempt to avoid typographical complications in this text I would like the reader to envisage the phonetic emphasis as presented in the examples below:

PLAIN		EMPHATIC	
[ˈɟoːra]	marry (3rd P. F.)	[ˈɟõːrɑ]	husband
[pʰarˈpʰuːrɪ]	fluttering	[pʰɑrˈpʰũːrɪ̃]	blowing (the nose)
[ʔɪčča ˈbɪčča]	trivial minutia	[ʔĩttsĩ ˈʔĩttsɑ]	ninety nine
[ˈsaːɥa]	old	[ˈṣɑːwɑ]	thirst
[ˈsiːma]	silver	[ˈṣĩːmɑ]	fasting

ACKNOWLEDGEMENTS

This book is a gesture of love to my Assyrian people whose language has served the human knowledge for long centuries. Because I hate to see a language, any language, in danger of extinction, I spent years and years to document a certain aspect of my native tongue. Now that this book is no longer a dream, I must thank all those who, directly or indirectly, helped me in realizing the dream. Therefore, special thanks are extended across the Atlantic to my Professors Celia Scully and David Barber of Leeds University/England who supervised the initial research I conducted on Neo-Aramaic. Sincere thanks are also due to my friend Professor Dr. Wolfhart Heinrichs of Harvard University for his constructive criticism of an early version of my manuscript. I am equally grateful to Professor Dr. Otto Jastrow of Universität Erlangen-Nürnberg for evaluating my manuscript and accepting it for publication in his new series, Semitica Viva.

Deep gratitude is also due to two Assyrian institutions namely the Dr. David Perley Fund of Cambridge/Massachusetts, and the Assyrian Academic Society of Chicago both of which partially funded this publication. Loyola University of Chicago has also assisted in covering the expenses of typing the manuscript.

Finally, I have not to forget to extend my love and appreciation to my wife and my son who were too patient to disturb me while the book was being written.

Chicago, March 1987   Edward Y. Odisho

INTRODUCTION

This study is basically a description of the phonetics and phonology of a certain dialect of the Neo-Aramaic language which is identified as the *NA Koine of the Assyrians in Iraq*. Several treatises have been written on NA, in general, most of which emphasize its historical development, morphology, grammar and lexicon. Oftentimes, the phonetics and phonology are contracted into a few pages that are insufficient to give a comprehensive and detailed picture of this particular linguistic level. Therefore, by limiting the domain of this research, it has become possible to conduct a more exhaustive investigation, which, in turn, has led to a more systematic description of, at least, one variety of NA. Moreover, most of the phonetic description is based on experimental evidence obtained by means of a wide variety of experimental procedures commonly in use today in phonetic studies.

As a historical ethnolinguistic introduction to the more technical aspects of the book, the author could not avoid the treatment of the controversial issue of the historical origin of the speakers of this dialect who know themselves as *Athūrāye (Atūrāye)* or *Sūrāye* while the Iraqi Arabs recognize them as *al-Athūrīyūn* for which the English equivalent is "Assyrians."

Despite the addition of this background study, the book remains a compact synthesis of the research conducted in NA Koine of Iraq from 1973 through 1986.

CHAPTER I

AN ETHNOLINGUISTIC HISTORY OF ASSYRIANS

1.1. *The Neo-Aramaic Language*

Most investigators have dealt with NA as scattered dialects or vernaculars rather than as a language. This would have been true prior to the standardization of the Urmi dialect in the nineteenth century.[1] But since then a fairly uniform standard written language has been in circulation. In fact, the educated people, speakers of widely different regional dialects, use the written variety as a guide in oral communication. The situation in Aramaic today is not unlike that in other languages where a standard written form coexists with the dialects.

All Semitists treat NA as a descendant of Aramaic, but whether it is a direct lineal descendant of Syriac (a widely spread variety of Aramaic) or not, is a matter open for further discussion. According to Wright (1890:20), Syriac might have originated from the dialect of the district around Orhai or Edessa. Maclean (1895:X) goes further to state that the modern vernacular is probably not derived from the Classical Syriac.

Using the prefix "Neo" does not mean that the language is a recent creation. NA is new only in its written version; otherwise, as a vernacular, its history seems much longer. This uncertainty about the origin of NA, together with the religious, ethnic and geographical connotations of the terms "Syriac" and "Syrian," which latter in Iraq refers essentially to a certain Christian denomination (Jacobite), are reasons for shunning the term "Syriac" and adopting Aramaic[2] instead, as the latter has been used to embrace many varieties of the old language. However, to bridge the temporal gap between the old and modern Aramaic, it would suffice to quote Krotkoff (1982:2) who states that:

The NA dialects are the surviving remains of the once widespread Aramaic language of antiquity. They are spoken by religious minorities in mountainous retreat areas and are divided into three main

---

1 Another less known written form of NA had apparently been created by the priests of the school of Alqosh since the seventeenth century or even earlier (Heinrichs, 1985).
2 It must be admitted that even "Aramaic" might not be absolutely appropriate due to its historical implications; however, it is helpful in clarifying certain facts and averting confusion between others.

groups: the westernmost Ma'lula group spoken in a few villages in Syria north of Damascus, the Turoyo group spoken in the area of Tur Abdin in eastern Turkey, and the easternmost group which is mostly identified with its main literary representative, the dialect of Urmi in northwestern Iran.

It is true that a cultivated form of Urmi dialect serves as the literary representative of the group, but one has to remember that the speakers of Urmi proper constitute only a small percentage of the total speakers of the dialects subsumed under this group.

Maclean (1895) divides the dialects of this group in the following manner:

a) The Greater Urmi dialects including Solduz, Sipurghan, Gavilan etc....
b) The Northern dialects which include Salamas, Qudshanis, Gawar, Jilu etc....
c) The Ashiret dialects which include Upper and Lower Tiari, Tkhuma, Tal, Baz, Mar Bishu, Shamizdin etc....
d) The Southern dialects which include Alqosh, Telkief, Telesqof, Bohtan, Zakho etc....

A more general classification of the above dialects is the one based on the hardening or softening of /t, d/ i.e., realizing them as plosives or as the interdental spirants (fricatives) /θ, ð/, a phenomenon that some writers (Maclean, 1895) designate as "aspiration." In modern phonetic terminology, it is quite misleading to realize the difference between the above two pairs as aspiration. Aspiration is a phenomenon that sets different categories of sounds, especially the plosives (stops), apart. It is the outcome of the difference in synchronization between the glottal and the supraglottal maneuvers; a difference that results in the absence or presence of a puff of air when the sound is articulated. The presence of the puff is usually marked by a superscript "h", thus /p^h, t^h, k^h/ are aspirated sounds while /p, t, k/ are unaspirated. The conversion of /t, d/ to /θ, ð/ represents *spirantization*. Spirantization will reduce almost all NA dialects to two groups which we prefer to label as /t, d/ dialects and /θ, ð/ dialects. Only few dialects violate this dichotomy when, for instance, /θ, ð/ are replaced with /s, z/, respectively.[3] Among the largest and best known /θ, ð/ dialects are those of Tiari, Tkhuma, Mar Bishu and Alqosh. Of interest here is that the Koine is a /t, d/ dialect and is currently exerting great pressure in despirantizing the aforementioned dialects.

---

3 The Jewish NA of Zakho (Sabar, 1974) and the unreported Christian NA of Suleimaniyah (Iraq) typically represent this substitution.

1.2. *Aramaic Language But Assyrian Descent*

The term "Assyrian" has always been the cause of endless controversy when used to designate a major group of the speakers of NA, the crucial question being whether the modern Assyrians are the descendants of the ancient Assyrians. The answer to this question should, at least, be twofold as reflected in the title of this section: A- linguistic and, B- historic and ethnic. A- Linguistically, the term sounds misleading when used to designate the origin of the language spoken by modern Assyrians. In modern linguistic literature, the Assyrian language is classified among the extinct North-East Semitic languages whereas the one spoken by the Assyrians today is traced back to Aramaic thus a North-West Semitic language. Sprengling states, "The language is clearly not that long dead tongue which we modern Westerners are accustomed to designate by that name, i. e., Assyrian" (*Introduction to Oraham's Dictionary,* 1943). B- Historically and ethnically Sprengling admits that "those people are probably as much descendants of ancient Assyrians as anything else" (ibid). Rogers (1915:302) strongly subscribes to this view; he states:

> The civilization of Assyria and Babylonia and their great sweep of history were not made by one people. Men of several different stocks contributed to the result, and here, as often afterward in the world's history, the history bears the stamp not of unity but of a diversity of races. Even in modern times, with all the resources at our command, it is often difficult to distinguish the different strains of races and to trace their influence in the movements of history. We need, therefore, feel no surprise that there should be great difficulty in tracing out the racial affinity of the peoples who made history in Assyria and Babylonia.

But even if one admits that the language of the modern Assyrians is Aramaic, the admission should not preclude the likelihood of a racial and historical affinity to the old Assyrians because historical identity and language are not inseparable. People can learn new languages and even nations can undergo a change of language (Burling, 1970). If the Irish, Scots and Welsh speak English today instead of their native Celtic languages it should not mean that they are Anglo-Saxons. This entails that massive linguistic conversions are not unfamiliar in the history of peoples and nations. To argue in favor of a historical relationship between the old Assyrians and the modern ones does not seem absurd and should not be seen as the outgrowth of a sentimental urge. It is simply an objective attempt to shed light on a controversial issue. The attempt is made in terms of three drastic changes and conversions, namely,

1.2.1. The Geopolitical Reshuffle
1.2.2. The Linguistic Shift
1.2.3. The Religious and Cultural Conversions

1.2.1. The Geopolitical Reshuffle

The argument here is based on the assumption that the downfall of Nineveh in 612 B.C., should not be envisaged as the total destruction of the Assyrian people. It is unreasonable to interpret the collapse of a political system in the sense of the instantaneous disappearance of its citizenry in its entirety. Nothing of this sort has happened in history and the survival of the citizenry of the Byzantine, Roman and Ottoman empires serves as best evidence in this regard. In each case it was the political machine that collapsed and the territory under its jurisdiction split into smaller countries, states or provinces that survived under the same or different names. This has to be so and cannot be otherwise, because those who perish with the collapse of the political system represent the minority while the majority outlives the collapse though frequently undergoes various political, religious and linguistic changes.

Sidney Smith is one of the few historians who does not readily accept the notion that the fall of Nineveh was the doom of the Assyrian people. Even though he finally accepts the notion, his choice of words and his argumentation are not indicative of a strong conviction in his conclusion. He first emphasizes the fact that after the fall of Nineveh some Assyrians i.e., part of the army managed to escape (from Nineveh) and take refuge in Harran where Ashur-Uballit was appointed King of Assyria (Smith, 1960:130). It is true that his kingdom lasted on until 605 B.C., but the very idea that some Assyrians did escape from Nineveh should imply that other Assyrians, in fact in greater numbers, must have also escaped from the rest of the major Assyrian cities or simply remained in their remote settlements. Later on he states that:

The disappearance of the Assyrian people will always remain an unique and striking phenomenon in ancient history [our emphasis]. Other similar kingdoms and empires have indeed passed away, *but the people have lived on* [our emphasis]. Recent discoveries, have, it is true, shown that poverty-stricken communities perpetuated the old Assyrian names at various places, for instance on the ruined site of Ashur, for many centuries, but the essential truth remains the same. A nation which has existed two thousand years and had ruled a wide area, *lost its independent character* [our emphasis]. (Ibid.)

The last sentence indicates that Smith tends to be more specific in the use of his terminology when he describes the whole event as the loss of the independent character of a nation which in our interpretation stands for the collapse of the political system rather than the disappearance of the people. If Smith admits that Arbela, which was not far away from Nineveh and Ashur, has escaped pillage why should he not concede that many other cities, especially in the remote and mountainous areas had, likewise, escaped pillage and slavery and their people survived though not necessarily as a political entity. Diakonoff distinctly rejects the notion of annihilation. He states:

The Assyrian people was not annihilated; it merely merged with the mass of Near Eastern Arameans, for as a result of the numerous deportations carried out by the Assyrian kings, Aramaic had long become the *lingua franca* of the ordinary people all over the Assyrian empire. (Diakonoff, 1985:124)

If such reasoning is rejected, then one is entitled to ask why of all the empires and kingdoms of the world which had collapsed, it is only the people of Assyria that had disappeared immediately while other peoples have survived the collapse of their political systems. It is my belief that the confusion between the annihilation of the Assyrian political system and the annihilation of the Assyrian people has emanated from Prophet Nahum's words. It is, therefore, unfortunate that many writers on ancient history regurgitate the prophecy without objective scrutiny and interpretation. It is also inconceivable that many writers quote Nahum, but only few quote Eskiel "who paints a more attractive picture of the Assyrian empire" (Saggs, 1962:240). It is even more inconceivable that so many writers single out the ancient Assyrians as barbarians, while few reveal that the Biblical condemnation of them is more because of their arrogance and their failure to recognize and acknowledge the source of the power they wielded by God's will than because of any specific aspect of their treatment of subjects or conquered races (p. 239). It is, in fact, absolutely inconceivable that "there be so much distorting over-emphasis upon the occasional atrocities" (Saggs, 1973:171) of the Assyrians, while other aspects of the Assyrian character be obscured (Saggs, 1962:240). For instance, there is little mention of their administrative efficiency, their artistic achievement, their innovation in designing irrigation systems, and their founding of the first library in the history of the human race. It suffices to say that it was the function of Assyria to safeguard the civilized world against the tribal hordes viz., Mushku, Medes, Cimmerians, Scythians, Hyksos, and Haribu who could have spread havoc and terror in the region and could have caused an early breakdown of civic order (Saggs 1973:171) "This [argument] is not to deny that the Assyrian administrative methods were by modern standards harsh, but the other sides of the system must not be overlooked" (Saggs, 1962:240). What is striking is that there seem to be some sharply contrasting views that need to be readdressed more objectively in order to arrive at a more realistic and convincing picture. Consequently, and in the light of this perspective to the nature of the Assyrian empire and its people, any fiery and exaggerated statements about the sudden evaporation of the Assyrian people should be rejected. To state that

Nineveh was laid waste and all the population was slaughtered or slaved... At one blow Assyria disappeared from history... Nothing remained of her except certain tactics and weapons... Not a stone remained visible of all the temples... (Durant, 1942:283–84)

have no place in an objective assessment of history. Such statements could be typical of a romantic narration of history but never a realistic one. It is true that Nineveh, as a capital, fell. It is true that Assyria, as a political system, collapsed. It is also quite conceivable to talk of tens, or even hundreds of thousands of casualties. But none of the above facts should be construed as the total annihilation of the Assyrians. Other than those hundreds of thousands who perished the rest of the Assyrians remained there or, at most, were "scattered upon the mountains" as Prophet Nahum foretells.

It is appropriate here to draw an analogy with World War II. In the recorded history of humanity there has been no worse catastrophe than this war. Berlin was destroyed, millions of soldiers and civilians did perish and the Nazi war machine and regime did disintegrate, but the German people and Germany survived though in two parts and with many other small parts being annexed to the neighboring nations.

Of greater significance in this discussion is the fact that after the downfall of Assyria another entity emerges under the name of *Athura* which seems to stand for a reduced form of the Assyrian province.

Athura satrapy in the Behistun royal inscriptions of King Darius (558–486 B.C.) is translated as "Assyria" (Rawlinson, 1859; cf. Olmstead, 1948; Cook, 1983, 1985). According to Cook, "the name Athura itself implies the Assyrian homeland on the Middle of Tigris and it continued to be so named for centuries surviving in Strabo as 'Atouria'" (Cook, 1983:81). On the other hand, Cook is not certain as to what Athura precisely meant to the Achaemenids; consequently, he suggests that "the ethnic Athuriya comprised Assyrians/Syrians of the former Assyrian kingdom which the Medes would have known as distinct from Babylonia" (1985:262). However, Cook does stress the fact that Athura appears in the original list of satrapies of the time of Darius' accession when Abarnahra (Ebirnari) was not a separate satrapy (ibid.).

In his description of the Persian army, which was recognized according to nationality, Herodotus (484–425 B.C.) mentions the Assyrians as a nationality in the army. He states "These people used to be called Syrians by the Greeks, Assyrian being the name for them elsewhere" (Herodotus, *Histories*, VII, 63).[4] Interesting in this regard is Rawlinson's statement that "*Syrian* and *Assyrian* are in reality two entirely different words. Syrian is nothing but a variant of *Tyrian*. The Greeks when they first became acquainted with the country between Asia

---

4 Rawlinson (1859:51) renders the quotation as "This people whom the Greeks call Syrians are called Assyrians by the Barbarians."

Minor and Egypt found the people of Tyre (Tzur) predominant there, and from then called the country in which they dwelt Syria" (Rawlinson, 1859:52).

Later in history, particularly during Alexander's invasion of the Middle East, the name of the region recurs as *Aturia* in the narrations of the Greek historians to denote the region of Nineveh (Herzfeld, 1968:305). Elsewhere, Aturia is meant to stand for the district between the Tigris and the Gordyean mountains (Jouguet, 1928:31). In the *Encyclopedia Americana* (1982, II:166), one reads that

> Adiabene was an ancient kingdom lying between the Tigris River and the two of its tributaries, the Greater and the Lesser Zabs. At one time it included all of Assyria proper and the Mesopotamian province of Nisibis and the district of Ecbatana. In 116 A.D., the country was conquered by Trajan, who made it a Roman province under the name Assyria. Hadrian, however, allowed it to resume its autonomy under the Parthian suzerainty. The capital of the Kingdom was Arbela. (Cf. Paulys Realencyclopädie, 1893)

Quoting Andrae (1938) and Smith (1926), Crone and Cook (1977:55–56) summarize the history of the Assyrians and Assyria during the Parthian and Sasanian rules as follows:

> Assyria which had neither the fabled wealth nor the strategic importance of Babylon, had been left virtually alone by the Achaemenids and Seleucids; condemned to oblivion by the outside world, it could recollect its own glorious past in a certain tranquillity. Consequently, when the region came back into focus of history under the Parthians, it was with an Assyrian, not a Persian let alone Greek, self-identification. The temple of Ashur was restored, the city was rebuilt, and an Assyrian successor state returned in the shape of the client kingdom of Adiabene. The Sasanids put an end to the autonomy of this kingdom, but they did not replace the local rulers with a Persian aristocracy; though reduced to obedient servants of the Shahanshah, a native aristocracy therefore survived.[5]

Smith's (1926:69) introductory notes on Unvala's edition and translation of the Pahlavi text entitled *Drakht i Asurik* (The Assyrian Tree) includes the following paragraph which is, to a great extent, consistent with the above information regarding the presence of the Assyrians. He states:

> The Assyrian *capital,* Nineveh, fell in 612 B.C.; the last effort of the Assyrians for independence failed at Harran in *circa* 610 B.C. In Achaemenian times there was an Assyrian detachment in the Persian army but they could only have been a remnant. That remnant persisted through the centuries to the Christian era, and continued to use in their personal names appellations of their pagan dieties. This continuance of an Assyrian tradition is significant for two reasons. The miserable conditions of these late Assyrians is attested by the excavations at Ashur and it is clear that they were reduced to extreme poverty under Persian rule.[6]

---

5 In the North, Assyria was literally resurrected: Nuzi, Kakzu, Shibanniba were inhabited again, and Asur, rebuilt anew, became at least as large a city as it had been in the heyday of the Assyrian empire (Roux, 1964: 351).

6 According to Colledge (1967:95) at Assur, a shrunken community of Assyrians survived. There they continued to worship their god Ashur and his consort and as late as A.D. 200–228, they were still using such grand old personal names as Sinaheerba and Esarhaddon.

With the spread of Christianity, it becomes more difficult to adduce more tangible evidence about the Assyrians as a socio-ethnic entity or people because of their adoption of Christianity through the medium of the Aramaic language which had already been dominant in Assyria and all over the Middle East and which was later known as Syriac. Nevertheless, there are hints and clues embedded here and there which when integrated together could shed further light on the survival of Assyrians. It is reported that "Tatian, the author of the Diatessaron in the second century A.D., called himself an 'Assyrian,' that is, he came from Assyria, the land between the Tigris and Media on the west and east, and the Armenian mountains and Ctesiphon on the north and south, probably from Adiabene" (Vööbus, 1951:10). In the *Ancient Syriac Documents,* a mention is made of the disciples of Addai who return to "their own country of the Assyrians" in the time of Narsai "the king of the Assyrians'" (Cureton, 1864:16). At the time of Julian the Apostate (A.D. 332–363) there was one Sanherib, King of Athor, a magian whose son converted to Christianity (Bedjan, 1890–1897, II:401). In the *Acta Mar Kardaghi,* it is mentioned that Shapur II invited Mar Kardag, of great royal race, a descendant of Nimrod and Sennacherib to the Persian court and appointed him *Marzban* (the military governor) of Assyria for the Sasanids until his conversion (Abbeloos, 1890:12).

"When Rome conquered Syria and north Mesopotamia, and only south Mesopotamia remained in the possession of the Arsacids (Parthians), another shift took place: the region (south Mesopotamia) became attached to Babylonia and this received the official name *Asuristan*" (Herzfeld, 1968:307). Apparently, this designation of Asuristan remained throughout the Sasanid rule and until the Moslem conquests. This fact is documented in the inscriptions of *Ka'be-yi Zardusht* which indicate that the fifth province of the Sasanian empire is called Asuristan (Britannica/Macropaedia, 1985:847).

The crucial question here is why the region was called Asuristan and not Babylonia which was geographically more appropriate. Is it because the northeastern part of the ancient Assyria was known as Adiabene, thus extending the designation of Asuristan to include south Mesopotamia and also because the Persians continued to identify the few millions[7] of Aramaic-speakers as Assyrians contrary to the Greek and Roman tradition of substituting Syrian for Assyrian? It is difficult to determine the real cause of the renaming; however, it seems plausible to deduce that names associated with Assyria were not void and had not fallen into obsolescence.

---

7 Arabic traditions estimate that in the caliphate of Umar I, the population of Aramaic-speakers in Sawad of Kufa only was about one million and a half (Morony, 1984:175).

1.2.2. The Linguistic Shift

In order to understand the nature of this shift and the manner in which it functioned, the following five points are worthy of consideration:

A. Before and after the downfall of the Assyrian empire there were no clear-cut political or geographic boundaries between the Assyrian and Aramean provinces. There was always a great deal of territorial overlap between those two entities. For instance, the cities of Nisibis (Nisibin), Orhai (Edessa) and Harran, which were centers of Aramaic language, had been regions within the Assyrian empire (Rogers, 1915; Oppenheim, 1967). In fact, those cities alternately belonged to the Assyrian empire and the Aramean states.

B. The Aramaic language was the *lingua franca* of the Middle East.

During the second millennium B.C. various Aramaic dialects are likely to have been spoken at the borders and within Mesopotamia and the Fertile Crescent. But it was the dialect used by the Arameans settled within the confines of Assyria that from the eighth century (B.C.) on supplanted all other dialects. (Rosenthal, 1974:6)

In the declining years of the Assyrian empire it (Aramaic) was evidently very widely spoken and written there (Kraeling, 1969:5). In fact it survived the falls of Nineveh (612 B.C.) and Babylon (539 B.C.) and remained the official language of the Persian empire (538–331 B.C.) (*Encyclopedia Americana*, 1982, II:168). Concerning its status under the Achaemenids, Frye (1963:99) points out that

By the time of Darius Akkadian (Assyrian/Babylonian) was all but a dead language used only by scribes and priests. Already under the Assyrians, Aramaic, with its alphabet, had displaced Akkadian as the *lingua franca* of the Near East. The Achaemenids apparently supported the use of Aramaic as the general means of communication in their empire.

If the Assyrians were attacked from the East and South, they had no route for retreat other than in the direction of the West and North. This pattern of retreat would most likely mean a greater merger with the Arameans. Some go to the extent of claiming that Assyria was absorbed into the Aramaic-speaking world (Postgate, 1977; Diakonoff, 1985). A similar view postulates that with the fall of Assyria and the destruction of the Assyrian aristocracy, the Arameans virtually took over Mesopotamia (Kraeling, 1969:6). Of interest in this regard is that the Aramaic script was often called "Assyrian." Greenfield believes that

this appellation attests to the continued awareness that Aramaic developed into an independent entity during the Assyrian period. Greek writers use the designation *Assyria (or Syria) grammata* for Aramaic script when they refer to inscriptions in Aramaic ... At a later date, *Ketab Ashuri* (Assyrian script) is used in Talmudic literature for the "square" Jewish script which replaced the ancient Hebrew script. (Greenfield, 1985:710)

C. The Assyrian and Aramaic languages should not be envisaged as two drastically different linguistic systems. A more realistic look at the Semitic languages of that time would be to treat them as gradient systems on a continuum rather than as polar systems on the same continuum. It is not unreasonable to assume that most Semitic languages, especially those adjacent to each other, developed some sort of a "common language" and had at one time maintained a reasonable degree of mutual intelligibility. For instance, the Late Babylonian language is largeley characterized by Aramaic syntax with Babylonian words (Lambert, 1973:181). Besides, the knowledge of more than one language would have been very likely in ancient Mesopotamia. Hence, it is quite conceivable to think of Mesopotamia as an extensive bilingual or even multilingual community where people were vulnerable to language shift. It was these conditions that facilitated the shift from Sumerian to Akkadian and from Akkadian to Aramaic.

D. Another factor that contributed to the linguistic shift was the writing system. The cuneiform writing was a symbol of the Mesopotamian civilization. When the Aramaic language penetrated the region, it also brought with it an alphabetic script which far surpassed the cuneiform tradition in many respects. For instance, instead of the six hundred signs required for the cuneiform writing, Aramaic brought only twenty-two letters which made recorded communication far more practical (Saggs, 1962:153). Thus Aramaic spread downstream into the heartland of Mesopotamia slowly, but inevitably, sapping the strength of the old cuneiform scribal tradition of that region (Oppenheim, 1964:60). To be more specific, it was amongst the learned that cuneiform writing remained in use for scholarly and esoteric purposes for some centuries more. By 140 B.C., it had completely disappeared except amongst a few priests who employed it for religious purposes for another half century, and among astronomers (Saggs, 1962:153). This is consistent with Toynbee's statement that in the last century B.C., the Akkadian language and cuneiform script had become extinct throughout their Mesopotamian homeland (Toynbee, 1947:19).

From its inception, the Aramaic alphabet, in a sense, had to fight a duel with the cuneiform system of writing. It was a long struggle – it lasted until the commencement of the Christian Era – between the complicated theocratic system of writing accessible only to certain privileged classes and the simple democratic system accessible to everybody; at the end of the seventh century B.C., all Syria and a great part of Mesopotamia became thoroughly Aramaized (Diringer, 1968:200).

This linguistic shift had many major consequences. The refusal of the Arameans to accept the Mesopotamian way of writing retarded the expansion of the Assyrian and Babylonian civilization (Oppenheim, 1967:34–35). It also caused the loss of a salient feature of that civilization and the disruption in the continuity of a tradition so characteristic of it. Most important of all, it accelerated the spread of the Aramaic (Syriac) language and the overall linguistic conversion to the extent that "the Greeks developed the habit of describing all Aramaic-speakers as Syrians" (Bosworth, 1980:292).

Thus the territorial overlapping between the Assyrians and Arameans, the linguistic affinity between their languages and the role of Aramaic as a *lingua franca* of the region would make the linguistic shift highly likely. In fact, the collapse of the political system in Assyria helped only to accelerate the shift.

E. Linguistically, the jumble of names used to identify the modern Assyrians (Asūristānyī, Athūrāyā, Atūrāyā, Sūrāyā, Suryāyā, Athūrī, Ashūrī, Asūrī etc.) could be traced back to the same root. With a bit of linguistic knowledge, the differences between those names will turn out to be superficial and the result of phonetic and morphological differences across languages. If, for instance, the adjectival suffix is deleted, we are left with a root that displays a mere phonetic difference essentially confined to the interchange between /š, s, θ, t/. This phonetic change is common across languages. Notice that:

š → s	is common in certain languages e. g., Proto-Semitic → Arabic. The change is also necessary in the Greek rendition of foreign words containing /š/ as Greek has no /š/ sound.
θ → s	is very common in languages that do not have the interdental fricative pair /θ, ð/ as is the case in most languages of the world including the local languages of the Middle East: Turkish, Persian, Kurdish and some NA dialects.
θ → t^h	is an alternative and equally common change to the above one. It is typical in NA dialects most of which, as a rule, replace the /θ, ð/ with /t, d/, respectively.
θ → š	is common with the major Tiari dialects of NA.

As for the deletion of the initial "a" in some of the forms, it could represent another morphological difference that has developed and spread through Persian, Greek or Armenian. Herzfeld (1968:306) points out that many Old Iranian names appear with or without initial "a": Amadai > Māda; Amardoi > Mardoi; Ašimanu > Šimanu.

The above alternations are highly likely if one bears in mind that the original term, regardless of whether it was *Ashur* (as in Akkadian and Hebrew) or *Athur* (as in Aramaic and Persian), has moved from one Semitic language across to other Semitic or non-Semitic languages. According to the alternations, a Greek would most likely render [aššur] as "'Ασσυρία" from which the English terms "Assyria" and "Assyrian" are coined. [aθur] would become [asur] in Turkish,

Persian, Armenian etc. and hence the derivations Asuri and Asuristan. Even for many speakers of NA [aθur] is commonly realized as [at^hur] and hence the derivation Aturaya.

Onomastically, however, I agree with Heinrichs (personal communication) that the connotations of Ashur, Athura, Athuria, and Asuristan are different throughout history. Some of the connotations have already been mentioned earlier on. Despite the geographic and ethnic overlapping that those appellations could indicate, they, nevertheless, seem to share a core designation of what the Greek historians call διὰ τῆς 'Ασσυρίας "Assyria proper" (Bosworth, 1980:287) or ἡ λοιπὴ 'Ασσυρίη "what was left of Assyria" (Herzfeld, 1968:306). It is particularly the latter interpretation that appeals to me because geographically it could stand for Assyria proper, demographically it could mean what was left of the Assyrian population, while ethnologically it could mean the survival of their cultural heritage.

1.2.3. The Religious and Cultural Conversions

With the advent of Christianity, most of the Mesopotamian religious rituals and practices started to disappear. Even though it is difficult to think of the pre-Christianity Mesopotamia as a strikingly heterogeneous religious entity, it is yet easier to think that Christianity enhanced the religious homogeneity of the whole region and helped to obliterate much of the religious inconsistency and create social uniformity in the region. So even if one disagrees with Joseph's (1961:19) claim that with the inception of Christianity "there remained no ethnic and national distinctions to be traced" among the people of the region, one has to share with him his view in that "the Oriental Christians refused to refer to their heathen ancestors" to the extent that much of the evidence about their forefathers is missing. A major corollary to the relgous conversion was the increase in the popularity and spread of Aramaic at the expense of other languages, especially Akkadian (Assyrian), as Aramaic, and specifically its Syriac version, became the language of eastern Christendom. From this point in time, the Christians (Assyrians, Chaldeans, Syrians) of the region were known as Suraye/Suryaye (Syrians) in contradistinction to the pagans (Manna, 1900; Crone & Cook, 1977). In other words the term Suraye acquired the triple connotation of "Christians," "Speakers of Syriac," and "the Syrian culture," which, however, should not necessarily imply that the ethnic and historical relationships and affiliations totally disappeared.

It is true that the early Christian Church developed Eastern (Nestorian)[8] and

---

8 Nestorius became the bishop of Constantinople in the year 428. Strictly speaking, the Church of the

Western (Jacobite) branches with the former spreading eastward of Syria into eastern Anatolia, Kurdistan, upper Mesopotamia, and Persia and being identified as Assyrian, while the latter being identified as Syrian (Atiya, 1968:240). To be more specific, "there were two distinct versions of Christianity within the Nestorian church: on the one hand, the local church of Assyria, a chauvinistic assertion of a provincial identity; and on the other, the metropolitan church of Persia with its center in Babylonia, a cosmopolitan assertion of a gentile truth" (Crone & Cook, 1977:57). Concerning the religious and ethnic continuity of the Assyrians, Crone and Cook state

The history of Karkha de-Bet Selokh (Kirkuk) begins with the Assyrian kings and ends with the Assyrian martyrs: Sargon founded it and the martyrs made it a blessed field for Christianity. Likewise, in the seventh century before Christ all the world stood in awe of Sardana, and in the seventh century after Christ the saints took his place as the "sun of Athor" and the "glory of Ninve." (Ibid)

Thus there is strong evidence that the orientation of the beliefs of the Eastern Church was partly due to a logical reaction to the pressure of the dominant establishment. Crone and Cook are very convincing in their interpretation of the, then, recurrent interactions between the Assyrians and the Persians. They present the following argument:

Under the Parthians, the Shahanshahs tended to demand religious conformity in return for political significance; under the Sasanids they did so systematically, thus imposing a Persian truth on an Assyrian identity ... They (Assyrians) were faced with the choice between the rectification of genealogy and the rectification of faith ... The Assyrians stuck to their genealogy, but could not merely go heretical (become Zoroastrian) because even a heretical Zoroastrian was still conceptually a Persian, and vis-a-vis the Persians the Assyrians therefore needed a different religion altogether. On the other hand, even an orthodox Christian was still only a Greek by association; vis-a-vis the Greeks a heresy therefore sufficed. Consequently, after a detour via Judaism – the conversion of Izates II, king of Adiabene to Judaism was reedited as the conversion of Narsai of Assyria to Christianity –, the Assyrians adopted Christianity and found their heresy in Nestorianism. (1977:56)[9]

Another concomitant change related to religion and culture was the change in the proper names which is, in itself, a significant ethnic and national marker that can conceal the lineal linkage between two eras in the history of an ethnic group or

East was founded earlier than that; the seeds had been sown in Jerusalem during the Apostolic age (Atiya, 1968:239). The appellation "Nestorian" came to be used in official or semi-official documents of the Church only in the thirteenth century, when Mar 'Abd-Ishu, Metropolitan of Nisibis, formulated "The Orthodox Creed of the Nestorians" in the year 1298 (Badger, 1852:49–51).

9 "To be or not to be a heretic was a subjective judgment on the part of the majority. Since the majority in the Ecumenical Councils which decided such matters was Greek, those who revolted against the Greek ideas were branded as heretic" (Watt, 1974:259). Nestorianism was branded as a heresy mainly because it "insisted on the right of non-Greek linguistic and cultural minorities to express their Christian faith in a manner consonant with their special outlook and mentality" (ibid).

nation. The Biblical and other Christian names swept the entire region. The popular names became: Ishu, Abd-Ishu, Sabr-Ishu, Hanan-Ishu, Bakht-Ishu, Yuhannan, Ephrem, Addai and names like Ashur, Sargon, Sennacherib, Esarhaddon were almost condemned to oblivion. The Greeks, Persians, and Arabs all had their influence in this respect.

In the same manner that Christianity and the Syriac language replaced the existing religious, linguistic, ethnic, and national markers with a different set of markers, so did Islam and the Arabic language later on. Although no attempt was made by Muslim governments to exterminate the Christians (Haddad, 1970:8), large scale apostasy and conversions were inevitable in the course of several centuries.

Although Iraq became a predominantly Muslim country, its fate was still not an unrelenting Hagarization. In the first place, the surviving Christians remained Syrians; despite the early adoption of Arabic and the ultimate disappearance of Syriac as a literary language, Syriac survived as the liturgical language throughout the province and as a vernacular in the rural strongholds of the Assyrians. (Crone & Cook, 1977:87)

After the Mongol invasion of the Middle East, most of the remaining Christians, especially the Nestorians of Iraq, deserted the urban areas and took refuge in the highlands north of Mosul extending to the Hakkiari mountains; some of them fled even further to the east and settled in the plains of Urmia. They remained there in almost total geographic seclusion suffering from poverty and ignorance until they were "rediscovered" by the European missionaries in modern times (Atiya, 1868:276). The geographic isolation in the mountains after the Mongol invasion, and even before it, seems to be a major reason for the scanty information resources on the ethnic and historic origin and background of the inhabitants of those regions.

1.3. Concluding Remarks

The above discussion aimed at unravelling the nature of the geopolitical reshuffle and the linguistic, religious and ethnic blending and amalgamation that had repeatedly changed the picture of the Middle East, in general, and Mesopotamia, in particular. The Sumerians, Assyrians, Babylonians, Arameans, Greeks, Romans, Persians, Arabs etc. have all contributed to the development of that picture. At times, that contribution enhanced the diversity in its texture, while at others it concealed it. We need, therefore, feel no surprise that there should be difficulty in tracing out the racial affinity, or at least the historical affinity, of some of the people of today to the people who made history in Assyria and Babylonia.

It is evident from the above discussion that the historians who have dealt with the destiny and history of the ancient Assyrians fall into three categories: (a) Most of them claim an abrupt disappearance of the Assyrian empire and the annihilation of its people. For this group the very question of any successors to the Assyrians is vacuous. (b) Some of them tend not to subscribe to the claim of annihilation; instead, they speak in terms of the Assyrians merging with their contemporaries, especially the Arameans. (c) A few of them mention the destruction of the Assyrian empire as a politico-military system, but at the same time they talk about the continuation of the identity under the Christian aegis.

In this study, the claim of the first group of historians is rebutted partly because it confuses the issue of the collapse of the politico-military system with that of the annihilation of its people, and partly because there is no precedence in the recorded history that a people or nation was annihilated all of a sudden. The views of the other two groups are plausible not only because they stand on firmer logical premises, but also because they adduce a good body of information and evidence that is in favor of the continuity in the history of the Assyrians though under different identities brought about by abrupt military and geopolitical changes coupled with gradual large-scale, multi-phased, and multi-faceted processes of acculturation and assimilation. The processes of acculturation and assimilation are essentially demonstrated in the form of a linguistic shift from Akkadian (Assyrian) into Aramaic (Syriac), a religious conversion from Paganism into Christianity, and a cultural conversion from Mesopotamian into Suryane. Therefore, any mention of Suryane after Christianity should be interpreted as a continued survival of the Christians of Assyria, Babylonia and Syria. Thus Suryane functions as a generic term subsuming a combination of the Syriac language and the Christian religion and its culture. Suryane was such a broad and effective bond that it obliterated many of the pre-Christianity ethnic and historical differences between the Assyrians, Babylonians, and Arameans and streamlined them.

There is also evidence that the effects of assimilation in the pre-Christianity and post-Christianity periods had been more extensive and devastating in Syria and Babylonia than in Assyria. This could be attributed to the following factors: Firstly, Assyria, especially its mountainous region, was strategically less significant and less vulnerable to foreign armies; moreover, the mountains always provided the last minute shelter for geographic isolation and, hence, survival. Secondly, and as a corollary to the previous point, the region remained relatively less diversified ethnically. Thirdly, there survived a strong native (Assyrian) aristocracy peculiar to itself and very conscious of its past and proud of it. This implies, and convincingly so, that Nestorianism as a religious identity seems to be a continuation of the ethnic and historical presence of the remaining Assyrians and the Arameans with whom they merged. Joseph's statement that "While the name Chaldean was appropriated by the Uniats, the illustrious twin name Assyrian was in time applied to the Nestorians and that they accepted and used it from the end of the nineteenth century" (Joseph, 1961:13) does not seem definitive and is not utterly tenable and plausible. There is, at least, Tseretely (1978:16) who points out that "Those (Assyrians) who live in the Soviet Union call themselves Assyrians and their mother tongue, Assyrian, an appellation which occurs in 18th-century Georgian documents." In any case, even if Joseph's view, inasmuch as the dating of the "renaming" of the "Nestorians" is concerned, is accepted, one has to emphasize the fact that the term "Assyrians" or "Aturaye" was not affixed to people who were alien or unrelated to it. It was more of a rectification of the broad term Suraye/Suryaye (Syrians) to identify a portion of the pre-Christianity and early Christianity population that geographically and historically belonged to the region.

The main objective of this study is not the discovery of a blood relationship between ancient and modern people. It is merely an attempt at a more objective investigation of a historical problem. The study is based on the assumption that only political systems vanish suddenly, while people disappear gradually through acculturation and assimilation. It is, therefore, not outrageous to propose that the "rediscovered" Christians of the highlands of Turkey and the plains of Azerbaijan are historically affiliated with the ancient population of that region, namely, the Assyrians and the Arameans.

To claim that the Assyrians as a people evaporated suddenly lacks logic and objectivity, to deny a historical association between the ancient and modern Assyrians with no objective and comprehensive investigation amounts to naivety or a premeditated attempt of history distortion, but, most certainly, to try to be more authentic and conclusive in this particular issue, further research is indispensable.

CHAPTER II

STANDARD WRITTEN NEO-ARAMAIC LANGUAGE
AND SPOKEN KOINE

2.1. Introductory Remarks

The dialects of NA in Iraq are, unfortunately, best identified in non-linguistic terms. The Assyrian dialects are those used by the followers of the Church of the East (also known as Nestorians) and by those who were of such Christian denomination before they were converted into other denominations in the nineteenth century by the European missionaries. Other NA speakers are locally known as Chaldeans and Syrians. Using Maclean's classification of NA dialects (1895), the Assyrians would occupy the first three groups of dialects (see Chap. I:1.1), the Chaldeans and Syrians would occupy the fourth group, though the speech of the Iraqi Syrians is influenced by the western Classical Syriac and they also use the western (Jacobite) script in writing and print.

2.2. The Emergence of Standard Written NA Language

When the European missionaries settled in Urmia region, they found that the masses of the Assyrians were unable to understand their old language and the gap between their language and their daily speech had become too wide to be bridged. Furthermore, mutual intelligibility between the regional and the tribal vernaculars was diminishing. In order to remedy this situation the missionaries decided to reduce the local Urmi dialect to writing so as to serve as the language of Church and education. The choice fell on the Urmi dialect not because it was widely spread or accepted by other inhabitants or other regions and villages or because it maintained greater affinity to the old written language. The choice was merely because the missionaries happened to have most of their main headquarters there. Thus a Standard Written Language (SWL) was created. Among the most significant works was the translation of the Bible into SWL in the year 1836 by the American Presbyterian missionary, the Rev. Dr. Perkins (Maclean, 1895:X).

Different missionaries began to found schools in which SWL was taught. The educational enterprise expanded. By 1841, the American mission had opened 17 schools in 16 different villages, and in 1851, Mr. Stocking, superintendent of schools, reported the existence of 45 schools with 871 pupils of whom 203 were women (Waterfield, 1973:109). The work of the Archbishop of Canterbury's mission also expanded rapidly.

By 1888, the mission was responsible for high schools in Urmia, Superghan and Ardishai and 40 village schools of which 17 were in Turkey and the remainder in Persia. They had a total of 1,200 students and used a considerable number of Assyrian clergy to teach them. (Ibid)

At first, the most fortunate of all in learning the skills of reading and writing were the Urmians, the children of some of the affluent people from other regions and the children of the tribal chiefs. With the increase in the number of schools, educational opportunities became available for greater numbers. By and large, the Urmians were lucky enough to be looked upon as the elite of the Assyrian community not only because they were the first to have access to education but also because their dialect served as the medium for that. This advantageous position of the Urmians together with the later development in the structure of the Assyrian community led to the gradual consolidation of SWL first in Iran and Iraq and later throughout the world.

It must be emphasized, however, that the newly established SWL was not an exact replica of the Urmi dialect; elements from the old language and other spoken dialects were brought in when necessary. Many of the Persian, Turkish, and Kurdish loanwords which had already been commonly used in NA dialects found their way into SWL.

The emergence of SWL was a landmark in the history of NA. The change heralded a new era of hope in the survival of Aramaic. It was a great turning point with very profound and far-reaching consequences. Among the most significant consequences were: (a) people were further isolated from their old language and cultural and intellectual heritage; (b) prestige and exaggerated importance was granted to a dialect that was "the speech of only a small proportion of the people" (Maclean 1895:xii); (c) it helped this particular dialect to gain ground at the expense of other dialects as people began to acquire the skills of reading and writing; (d) it was the first step towards the evolution of a *lingua franca* dialect among the Assyrian speakers of NA in Urmia first and then the rest of the regions. It is this spoken variety which after World War I developed into a widespread Koine in Iraq.

2.3. *Further Development and Spread of the Koine*

In any war it is the weakest and the most deprived who suffer most and the Assyrians were not an exception to this detested war axiom. Due to various maneuvers by the Allies before and during World War I, the Assyrians "chose the harder way, and despite the instinctive warning of self-interest, they threw their lot with the Allies, for this they suffer today" (Murray, 1970:4). Fierce fighting erupted in their region and they had to evacuate their homeland once again after they had done so centuries ago at the hands of the Mongols.

Being open to ferocious attacks of the Turkish army and the local Kurds, huge waves of refugees began to leave the Hakkiari region towards Urmia where the situation became even worse. The whole Assyrian community turned into a refugee army. "The women and the children rode, some in little carts, some on mules, with scant supply of bread for their long journey to no destination" (Emhard & Lamsa, 1970:113). The march of some four hundred miles went from Hakkiari in Turkey, to Urmia, in Iran, then southwards to Hamadan then westwards across the Iraqi borders to Ba{c}quba near the northeast of Baghdad. Fighting, famine and epidemics annihilated tens of thousands of them – the author's mother was the only survivor from a family of five. Those who were lucky enough to survive the tragic march were sardined into refugee camps in Ba{c}quba.

The conditions of migration, though so pathetic, were the first large-scale opportunity for the reshuffling of speakers of all the regional and tribal dialects of Assyrians. At least some fifteen dialects are mentioned in Maclean's division of those dialects. Of course the number of dialects easily increases if more refined distinctions are marked. Maclean rightly points this out by saying that "almost any village has its own way of speaking" (1895:xii). A more accurate view of the dialectal diversity would be, and still is though to a lesser extent, in terms of "cluster dialects," i.e., each major regional (geographic) and tribal (social) dialect stands for a number of sub-dialects differentiated marginally according to the villages and clans. Even nowadays in Iraq, when Tiari is mentioned it would embrace Upper Tiari (Tiari Letha) and Lower Tiari (Tiari Xtetha) and the former would include Chammanayi, Waltwayi, Bne Rumtha, Sar Spidnayi, Dadushnayi etc. and the latter would include Ashithnayi, Bne Matha, Bne Belatha, Bne La Gippa, Zawitnayi, Minshayi etc. If Baz is mentioned it would embrace Shawitnayi, Mahayi, Artusnayi, Silimnayi etc. Very often the difference between some of those subdialects is easily noticed. Of all the countries where Assyrians live, Iraq encompasses a greater variety of dialects and subdialects that still maintain their distinct identities to a certain extent. Syria is another country where the dialects still have a distinct presence because the Assyrian refugees who left Iraq after the 1933 massacre of Simele were resettled along the Khabur river on the basis of their tribal affiliations. This pattern of settlement in the rural areas had two consequences: (a) it helped retain the dialects considerably intact; (b) it offered minimum opportunity for dialect interaction and, hence no common dialect (koine) evolved.

After the temporary settlement in Ba^cquba, a considerable number of the Assyrians moved to the villages in the North of Iraq. Some joined the British Levy Army in Habbaniyyah while others took jobs here and there. For those who settled in the urban areas, the tribal system and the village-based coherence began gradually to disintegrate. In the 1930s the number of the Assyrians moving to the urban areas began to increase.[1] In the 1940s and 1950s almost half of their population was dwelling in the three oil cities of Kirkuk, Mosul (Ain Zala) and Basrah and the capital Baghdad. Another enclave comprised the army servicemen, the civilian personnel and their families who were stationed in Habbaniyah, the site of the British air base. This was the pattern of their geographic distribution till the mid-1950s.

This geographical relocation after World War I did not only change the social and tribal stratification, it, in fact, greatly eliminated much of the dialectal differences between the Assyrians and pushed their spoken language towards uniformity. Being very keen on preserving their language, as part of their ethnicity, those few Assyrians who mastered the skills of reading and writing began to teach them to others in various ways that are typical of language minorities. The language was taught in a few private schools and churches. The parents and the older brothers and sisters taught it to the younger ones; in the absence of a literate person in the family, the children were sent to private tutors against nominal fees. By the end of the 1950s, a good number of Assyrians mastered SWL. The more they learned of it the more the tribal and the village dialects were dispensed with and a spoken Koine began to develop along the lines of SWL. The Koine became an acceptable medium of interdialectal daily communication.

What is noteworthy in this respect is that the Koine is neither the Urmi dialect nor a replica of SWL. It is a linguistic entity which is greatly influenced by both varieties but at the same time displays considerable divergence from them and the divergence is steadily growing. Although it is only a century and a half since the inauguration of SWL, it has now become a rather archaic linguistic entity compared to the Koine. SWL is currently used only in literature, teaching, religious services and formal speech acitivities. One would sound somewhat formal if he were to use SWL for daily communication.

---

1 Movement to the urban areas was mainly associated with the British business enterprises especially the oil industry.

2.4. Further Demographic and Social Changes and the Consolidation of the Koine

By the 1950s, when the Assyrians became more familiar with SWL and their regional and tribal intermingling reached its maximum, the Koine became a reality. However, the emergence of the Koine did not mean that the rest of the spoken dialects disappeared. On the contrary, most of the dialects and the subdialects were still in active circulation because of the geographic isolation of half of the Assyrian population in the rural areas, the survival of the first generation of urbanites, who were still speakers of native dialects and the existence of some small tribal pockets of population in the cities. Nevertheless, during the last twenty-five years, the Assyrian community as a whole has undergone two major changes that helped consolidate the status of the Koine. In 1958, the 14th July Revolution took place. Despite the chaos that ensued, the political transformation resulted in drastic educational and employment opportunities that led to the collapse of the older patterns of socio-economic, educational, racial and demographic stratifications in Iraq. The large cities became the meccas for the rural population including the Assyrians. What further expedited the migration of the Assyrians, in particular, was the eruption of the Kurdish revolt against the central government. Both events poured tens of thousands of Assyrians into the large cities thus bringing them into close contact with the Koine which is primarily an urban phenomenon. (For details see Odisho, 1984.)

Today the Koine is the predominant means of communication among the majority of Assyrians. The first generation has either vanished or is too old to exert any influence on the younger generations and the rural population has been reduced to a minimum. In both cases the regional and tribal dialects were rendered less influential and less resistant in the face of the Koine. It is difficult to exactly identify the users of the Koine. Nevertheless, one would confidently state that it is the speech of a considerable percentage of the urbanites, particularly those who were born in Iraq or were too young to exclusively acquire the dialect of their parents. In other words, it represents the speech of the second, third and fourth generations who grew up in Baghdad, Kirkuk, Habbaniyya and Basrah. Since the 1970s, more than thirty thousand Assyrians of Iraq have immigrated to the United States, Australia and some European countries. Does this then entail that the Iraqi Koine has been transplanted outside Iraq? The answer tends to be "Yes." Today, in Chicago, the Koine is rapidly gaining ground simply because the majority of the fifty thousand Assyrians living in this city are originally from Iraq and members of the above three generations.

It is relevant here to lay out the social structure of my own family to substantiate the significance of the collapse of the tribal relationships and endogamy in broadening the domain of the Koine. My father is from Lower Tiari (village of Zawita) and my mother is from the district of Urmia (village of Qara Jalu). We are five brothers, and except for two of us who are married to "German" and "Tiari" women, respectively, the rest of us are married to women whose original dialects are Jilu, Baz and Qudshanis. I have three sisters, two of whom are married to speakers of two different Baz dialects while the third is married to a speaker of the Ashitha subdialect of Tiari. And so the story goes on with some of the grandsons and granddaughters in the family. Except for one or two of the sons-in-law and daughters-in-law, who have, more or less, retained their original dialects fully or partially, the rest of us are typical representatives of Koine speakers. In fact, our Jilu sister-in-law sets an excellent example of bidialectalism, a linguistic phenomenon so common these days in the Assyrian community in Iraq. Whenever she stays with her parents, she speaks Jilu perfectly, but when she is back home or comes for a stay with my parents she shifts completely to the Koine with hardly any noticeable traces of her Jilu dialect. We should stress the fact that within the Assyrian community of Iraq, in particular, there are thousands of individuals who experience the same code-switching between two dialects one of which is the Koine, while the other is their native dialect.

2.5. *Some Salient Phonetic and Phonological Similarities and Differences Between the Koine and the Urmi Dialect*

As indicated in 2.3 above, the Koine is an offshoot of SWL and since the latter was essentially a formalized written variety of the Urmi dialect, it is quite natural, therefore, to find some aspects of similarity between the Koine and Urmi. They, for instance, share the following features:
(a) Both are /t, d/ dialects.
(b) Except for the greater tendency towards palatalization in Urmi, their basic consonantal systems, in terms of manner of articulation and place of articulation and consonant cluster formations, are very similar.
(c) Their vowel systems are mostly identical in that both have the same vowel quality range and have drifted along the same lines away from the traditional Aramaic vowel qualities. Typical in this respect is the emergence of the [e] and [o] vowels in the Koine and Urmi as opposed to the retention of [ay] and [aw(ʉ)], respectively, in the Ashiret dialects. Simultaneously, there is occasional replacement of [e] and [o] with vowels having a more close quality namely, [i] and [u]. (For details, see Chap. IV.)

(d) They both delete what Krotkoff (1982) calls the "m" prefix of the augmented verbal classes, a feature that is retained in traditional Aramaic and the Ashiret and Alqosh dialects. Notice the examples:

KOINE & URMI	TIARI	
+['ša:dɪr][2]	+['mša:dɪr]	send
['pʰa:rɪq]	['mpʰa:rɪq]	finish; save
['pʰa:rɪm]	['mpʰa:rɪm]	cut

The Koine, however, has diverged from the Urmi dialect in several areas the most important of which are:

(a) The Koine shows less pervasion of palatalization than in Urmi. In the latter, the palatal plosives [cʰ, ɟ] tend to be realized as the palato-alveolar affricates [čʰ, ǰ], while [čʰ, ǰ] shift forwards so as to sound like the alveolar affricates [ts, dz]. Notice the examples:

KOINE	URMI	
['cʰi:cʰa]	['čʰi:čʰa]	tooth
['cʰe:cʰa]	['čʰe:čʰa]	cake
['ɟɪlda]	['ǰɪlda]	skin; leather
['čʰamčʰa]	['tsamtsa]	spoon
['ǰaldɪ]	['dzaldɪ]	quick

(b) Also part of the palatalization tendency in Urmi is the diphthongization of long vowels. This is called palatalization because the monophthongal long vowels are shortened and then terminated with [y], a typical exponent of palatalization. Notice the examples:

KOINE	URMI	
['mdi:tʰa]	['mdiytʰa]	city
['ʔi:da]	['ʔiyda]	feast
['nu:na]	['nuyna]	fish
['zu:zɪ]	['zuyzɪ]	money

(c) [q] in the Koine retains its original Semitic phonetic nature as a voiceless unaspirated uvular plosive, whereas in Urmi it may shift into a voiceless unaspirated velar plosive [k]. Notice the examples:

KOINE	URMI	
[qa'la:ma]	[ka'la:ma]	pencil

---

[2] The phonetic and phonological status of emphasis will be dealt with later. At this stage, emphasis stands for the auditory feeling of thickening and darkening versus thinning and lightening of the sounds.

['ʔaqla]	['ʔakla]	leg
['qaltʰa]	['kaltʰa]	basket
['qla:pʰa]	['kla:pʰa]	peeling

(d) In Urmi the overall articulation of emphasis is less intense than in the Koine. The de-emphaticization tendency in the former could be attributed to the influence of Persian for which emphasis is an alien phenomenon. Nothing of this tendency is observed in the Koine because of its association with Arabic for which emphasis is most characteristic.

(e) The alphabet character ܘ 'waw' or the 'spirantized' ܒ̣ is essentially realized in the Koine as a labio-palatal approximant [ɥ] identical to the initial sound in the French word "huit" (eight). It changes into a labio-velar approximant [w], as in the French name "Louis" or the English pronoun "we" when it occurs in emphatic contexts or before back vowels. Notice the following plain and emphatic minimal paris:

ɥ		w			
['sa:ɥa]	old	+['sa:wa]	=	['ṣɑ:wɑ]	thirst
['ha:ɥi]	(they) be	+['ha:wi]	=	['ḥɑ: wĩ]	my air
['ʔi:ɥan]	I am (f.)	+['ʔi:wan]	=	['ʔĩ:wɑn]	proper name
['na:ɥɪ]	nits	+['na:wɪ]	=	['nɑ:wĩ]	well (gush) forth
['ɥa:da]	doing	+['wa:da]	=	['wɑ:ḍɑ]	promise; appointment

In Urmi, the phonetic realization of the same characters vacillates between a labio-dental approximant [ʋ] and a labio-dental fricative [v]. However, if we continue using "w" in our transcription it is only a typographical convenience. Therefore, the reader is advised to bear the phonetic difference between [ɥ] and [w] in mind because the former sound is highly characteristic for the sound system of the Koine.

(f) The medial sequence of geminated consonants in the Koine is reduced to a single consonant in Urmi. Notice the examples:

KOINE	URMI	
['lɪbba][3]	['lɪba]	heart
['dɪbba]	['dɪba]	bear
['šɪnnɪ]	['šɪnɪ]	years
['samma]	['sama]	poison

---

3 Since this is a synchronic comparison, no diachronic factors should be taken into consideration.

['šɪdda]   ['šɪda]   an evil spirit; monster

(g) Unlike the Urmi dialect, the Koine uses /y/ as the prefix of the general present indicative rather than /cʰ/. Notice the examples:

KOINE	URMI	
+['yaxla]	+['cʰaxla]	she eats
['yxazya]	['cʰxazya]	she sees
+['yy̌a:rɪb]	+['cʰy̌a:rɪb]	he tries
+['yqa:rɪm]	+['cʰqa:rɪm]	he wins

(h) Generally speaking, the Koine and Urmi seem to be influenced by the intonation patterns of Arabic and Persian, respectively. A major difference between their intonation patterns is confined to the interrogative sentences without question-words (i.e., the so-called non-wh-questions). In the Koine they are indicated by a rising pitch. Likewise, in Urmi the rise is there, but towards the end it converts into a level pitch.

Obviously, the similarities and differences are not restricted to phonetics and phonology; they involve all the linguistic levels including morphology, syntax and vocabulary. In fact, it is in their vocabulary that these two dialects are growing more dissimilar as Urmi has fallen under the influence of Persian while the Koine is strongly influenced by Arabic.

2.6. Inconsistencies Within the Koine

The attempt to introduce the Koine as a supposedly full-fledged dialect of NA in Iraq does not mean that it is a totally standardized, coherent and uniform system. In order for those features to materialize, at least three consecutive generations of speakers seem to be a prerequisite. The actual life-span of the Koine has barely exceeded three generations. In a hypothetical situation three generations are taken as a minimum time constraint for a complete shift from one language or dialect to another because the speakers of the first generation, whom we assume to be monolingual or monodialectal in the native linguistic system, will be neutralized by old age or death, the second generation will be bilingual or bidialectal while the third generation will be experiencing maximum displacement away from the native system. But because of other interferences, it is natural to expect a delay in the shift beyond the three-generations period. It all depends on how favorable the conditions are for a linguistic system to give in and for the other to overwhelm. This, in itself, is a problem of language maintenance and disappearance which is beyond the scope of this study. What would suffice to mention here is that the Koine has developed in the course of three generations but not without many inconsistencies in its linguistic system which indicate its lack of full standardization.

If one excludes the rural areas, where the Koine is non-existent, the situation of NA among the Assyrians in the urban areas is that of co-existence between the Koine and other tribal dialects. The co-existence is a transitional phase leading to the final phase of supremacy of the Koine because it is already in a very strong position and is socially the most prestigious dialect in Iraq. The co-existence has been brought about by the following three factors:

(a) Slow and limited exposure to the Koine of people who have been inhabiting the urban areas but still being confined, more or less, to tribal enclaves or pockets.

(b) The leading role of the second generation in the Assyrian community. Members of this generation have not managed to free themselves fully from the influence of the tribal/regional dialects as they grew up in intimate association with the first generation.

(c) The recent exposure of the post-1960s waves of rural migrants to the Koine.

The above three factors justify the description of the Koine as partially lacking in linguistic homogeneity, a condition which in essence means that certain speakers of the Koine still manifest indices of their tribal dialects. These indices are associated with pronunciation (phonetics and phonology), morphology, syntax, vocabulary etc. The inconsistency in pronunciation and vocabulary is more conspicuous than at other levels.

Before we proceed to elaborate on the differences in pronunciation, it is instructive to introduce specimens of words which are typically representative of the Koine lexicon but are frequently substituted with synonyms that are more representative of the tribal/regional dialects.

KOINE		TRIBAL/REGIONAL	
+[baˈɟiːra]	weak; slim	[laˈwaːza]	
or		([laˈqaːza])	
[ˈzabbun]			
[ˈbiːnisanɪ]	spring	[ˈbahar]	
[bašˈlantʰa]	kitchen	+[ʔašpasˈxaːna]	
or			
+[ˈmatbax]			
+[ˈbarcʰawɪtʰra]	afternoon; evening	+[ʔaˈsɪrtʰa]	afternoon; evening
		+[ˈbermaːšɪ]	evening

[ˈbnoːši]	alone (1st. P)	[ˈlxoːði] ([ˈlxuːdi])	
[ˈbraːtʰa]	girl	[ˈyaltʰa]; [ˈcɪččɪ]	
[ˈbrɪxša]	traveling; going	[ˈsyaːqa]	traveling (going northwards);
		+[ˈslaːya]	traveling (going southwards);
		[biˈzaːla]	going
[ˈɟaːyɪ]	time e.g., one time	[ˈbeːna] ([ˈbiːna]); [ˈnaqla]	
[ɟumˈbultʰa]	marble (game)	[tʰaˈballa]	
[ˈɟiːba]; [ˈdɪpʰna]	side	[ˈɟoːtʰa] ([ˈɟuːtʰa])	
[ˈǰaldɪ]	fast	[qaˈluːla]	
+[ǰɪˈɟaːra]	cigarette	+[ˈpaprus]	
[ˈǰundi] or [ˈʔascar]	soldier	+[ˈsaldat]; +[ˈsarbaz]	
[ġziː]; [ˈɟašɪq]	see; look	+[riː]; [ˈmtʰaːpʰɪtʰ]; [xur]	
[darˈbaːna]	wounded	[ˈbrɪndar]	
+[ˈdolma]	a dish (vineleaves, cabbage, onions stuffed with rice & ground meat etc.)	[ˈpʰraːxɪ]	
[hamˈzamtʰa]	talk; conversation	+[soːtʰa] (+[ˈsoːθa]) (+[sawˈwattʰa])	
+[zɪrˈqɪtta]	wasp	[dɪbˈbuːra]; +[zaˈrɪqta]	
[xamˈxuːmɪ]	having fever	[mšaˈθoːnɪ]	
[ˈxačča]	a little	[ciːm]	
+[ˈxoːra]	friend	+[ˈdosta]: +[ˈxawra]	
+[ˈxurmɪ]	dates	[ˈqazbɪ]	

[ˈxpaːqa]	lap	[ˈqapʰla]	
[ˈxaːna]			
[ˈxpaːqa]	embracing	[ˈqpʰaːla]	
[cɪrˈtoːpɪ]	potatoes	[paˈtaːtɪ]	
or			
[kɪrˈtoːpɪ]			
[ˈcʰɪrya]	short	[daˈqiːqa]	
[cʰɪšˈmiːšɪ]	raisins	[yaˈbiːšɪ]	
+[ˈcʰoːmɪr]	charcoal	+[ˈšɪxra]	
[ˈcʰušti]	wrestling	[ˈjdaːla]	
+[maˈhaːna]	excuse; pretext	[ˈxušta]	
[maˈcʰuːsɪ]	covering	[mcʰaˈpʰoːyɪ]	
+[mɪrya]	sick	[ˈnaxoš]; ([ˈnaxwaš]); [ˈʔaːjɪz]	
[mɪsˈciːna]	poor; humble	[pʰaˈqiːra]	
[ˈmiːxa]	nail	+[bɪsˈmaːra]	
[naˈnuntʰa]	grandmother	[ˈtoːta]; [soˈtʰuntʰa]	
[ˈnoːba]	turn	[ˈjarra]	
[ˈscɪntʰa]	knife (small and big)	[ˈscɪntʰa] +[ˈšapʰra]	small knife big knife
[spaˈdiːtʰa]	pillow	[baˈrɪšta]	
[ˈʔascar]	army	[ˈqoːšɪn]; ([ˈqoːšun])	
+[ʔazlaˈcʰuːšɪ]	spider	[zaqraˈqoːdɪ]	
+[ˈʔoyma]	dress	+[sudra]	
[pʰarxaˈleːlɪ]⁴	butterfly	[pʰarxaˈniːtʰa] ([pʰarxaˈniːθa])	
+[pʰalˈluːyɪ]	dividing (whole into two)	[ˈqsaːya]	
+[ˈpʰlaːta]	dislocation (bone)	[ˈšlaːpʰa]; [ˈxlaːya]	
+[ˈpʰraːta]	tearing	[ˈčʰraːta]; +[ˈsraːta]	

---

4 Oddly enough the etymology of the word stands for "to fly" + (at) "night."

+[saˈwa:na]	ugly	[ˈsirɣa];
		[ʔiˈba:ʝar];
		[ˈcʰra:yat]
+[saˈru:pʰa]	pungent	[ˈdɪzwar]
+[qaˈruwwa]	cock	[ˈdi:ca]
+[qaˈtʰɪrtʰa]	mule	[cʰoˈdɪntʰa]
		([cʰoˈdɪnθa])
		([cʰaˈwɪdna])
[ˈqudmɪ]	tomorrow	[ˈtʰɪmmal]
[ˈqudmɪ]	yesterday	[ˈtʰɪmmal]
[ˈqi:na]	green	[miˈla:na]
		(+[miˈla:na])
+[ˈqɪssa]	forehead	[biˈʔe:na]
+[ˈrumtʰa]	hill; high land	[ʝarˈrɪcʰtʰa]
		([ʝarˈrɪcʰθa])
[ˈri:ʝa]	servant	+[xuˈla:ma];
		+[qaˈra:waš]
[šaˈpi:ra]	handsome	[ˈǰwanqa];
		[laˈxu:ma]
[šaˈpɪrtʰa]	beautiful (f.)	[ˈxamtʰa]
		([ˈxamθa]);
		[laˈxumtʰa]
[šaˈxi:na]	hot	[xaˈmi:ma]
+[šayˈya:na]	adhesive	[dabuˈša:na];
		[dabuˈqa:na]
+[šra:ya]	lamp	[ˈlampʰa]
+[tʰa:ġar]	large water jar	[ˈli:na]
[tʰaˈlɪmtʰa]	small water jar	[ˈlɪntʰa];
		[zaˈwɪrtʰa];
		[cʰaˈwa:za]
[tʰaˈpʰu:xɪ]	spilling	+[mbaˈdu:rɪ];
		[ˈbya:za]
+[tʰumˈba:na]	trousers	[šɪrˈwa:la]
[ˈtʰarsa]	inside out	[ˈxɪrxɪt]
		([ˈxɪrxat])

2.6.2. Variations in Pronunciation

The variations in pronunciation are great in number and diverse in nature and are not all the result of inconsistency in phonetics and phonology; occasionally they are part of morphology. The use of [y] instead of [c^h] as the prefix of the general present indicative and the retention of the prefix [m] in the augmented verbal classes are morphological markers. They are, nevertheless, included here primarily because of their direct and significant impact on pronunciation.

Among the speakers of the Koine, sound deviations are easily distinguished and are, in fact, cumulatively treated as accent i.e., speaking the Koine with an accent. Neither the exponents of accent nor its acuteness are the same with all of the non-homogenized speakers of the Koine. Some display minimum accent which is difficult to detect, while others have a marked accent. As for the anomaly in pronunciation, it does not yield itself easily to a straightforward generalization. It could range from a slight difference in the articulation of certain segments (consonants and vowels) to a change in suprasegmental (prosodic) features. hence the changes may include occasional and/or systematic alternations, deletions or additions of sounds or classes of sounds, metathesis, presence or absence of emphasis, stress displacement and overall melody.

2.6.2.1. Variations in Sound Segments

Here are specimens of some of the most recurrent and characteristic deviations in sound segments which are treated as leftovers from tribal and regional dialects. It is beyond the scope of this study to determine the phonological status of those changes within the dialects compared to the Koine. What matters here are the overall realizations of phonetic inconsistencies within the Koine and the deviations from it. It should be emphasized that these deviations from the Koine are not necessarily encountered consistently nor are they always strikingly conspicuous. They are less so when the speaker is aware of the negative implications of failing to adopt the Koine. They are more so when the speaker is carefree and the situation is informal and there is no stigma attached to his native dialect. The greater the domination of the Koine in a certain urban concentration, the more the tribal and regional dialects are stigmatized. Traditionally, the mountainous dialects, viz. Tiari, Jilu, Baz, Mar Bishu, among others, were, and still are the victims of linguistic stigmatization. However, recently, dialectal differences are more tolerable due to the spread of education and a surge in nationalism.

The specimens from a specific dialect might not mean that they are restricted only to it; they are rather more characteristic of it.

2.6.2.1.1. Variations in Consonants

[tʰ] → [θ]⁵
[d] → [ð]

KOINE	TIARI	
[ˈxaːtʰa]	[ˈxaːθa]	new; sister
[ˈbeːtʰa]	[ˈbeːθa]	house
[ˈmaːtʰa]	[ˈmaːθa]	village
[ˈʝraːda]	[ˈʝraːða]	scraping
[ˈmaːqɪd]	[ˈmaːqɪð]	burn!
[ˈʝuːda]	[ˈʝuːða]	skin container (for churning milk)

[tʰ] → [š]

[ˈbeːtʰa]	[ˈbeːša] ([ˈbeːθa])	house
[tʰa]	[ša]	come!
[ˈcʰtʰeːtʰa]	[ˈcʰθeːša] ([ˈcʰθeːθa])	hen

[tʰ] → [y]

KOINE	JILU	
[ˈbeːtʰa]	[ˈbɪyya]	house
[cʰuˈsiːtʰa]	[kʰuˈsɪyya]	hat
[ˈcʰtʰeːtʰa]	[ˈkʰtʰɪyya]	hen

[q] → [k]
[cʰ] → [kʰ]
[ʝ] → [g]

[ˈʔaqla]	+[ˈʔakla]	leg
[ʔaˈqubra]	[ʔeˈkubra]	mouse
[ˈcʰtʰaːqa]	[ˈkʰtʰeːwa]	book
[ˈcʰuːpʰa]	[ˈkʰuːpʰa]	low
[ˈʝɪlda]	[ˈgɪlda]	skin; leather
[ˈʝumla]	[ˈgumla]	camel

KOINE	BARWAR	
[ˈʔiːcʰa]	[ˈʔeːkʰa]	where
[ˈducʰtʰa]	[ˈdukʰtʰa]; [ˈduːkʰa]	place

---

5 The direction of change is for descriptive purposes in this particular case and has, therefore, nothing to do with the historical change.

| ['ɟumla] | ['gumla] | camel |
| ['ɟılla] | ['gılla] | grass |

$[p^h] \to [f]$

['cʰe:pʰu]	['kʰe:fe]	his state (condition)
+['pʰayda]	['fayda]; ['fe:da]	benefit
+['pʰıllan]	['fıllan]	so and so (person)

$[ġ] \to [x]$

KOINE	TIARI	
+['pʰaġra]	+['pʰaxra]	body
+['ʔa:ġa]	+['ʔa:xa]	lord (feudalist)
+['darġa]	+['darxa]	rank

$[q] \to [tṣ]$

KOINE	BAZ	
+['qa:tu]	+['tṣa:tu]	cat
['qamxa]	+['tṣamxa]	flour
+[qır'ta:la]	+[tṣır'ta:la]	large basket
['qartʰa]	+['tṣartʰa] (+[tṣay'ruwwa])	cold

2.6.2.1.2. Variations in Vowels

$[e:] \to [ay]$

KOINE	BAZ	
['se:pʰa]	['saypʰa]	sword
['be:tʰa]	['baytʰa]	house
+['se:da]	+['sayda]	hunting

$[o:] \to [aw]$
$[ay] \to [e:]$

KOINE	TIARI	
['cʰo:sa]	['cʰawsa]	hair
['yo:na]	['yawna]	pigeon
+['so:ma]	+['sawma]	fasting
+['pʰayda]	['pʰe:da]	benefit

+['maydan]	['me:dan]	arena
+['ʔayna]	['ʔe:na]	eye
+['ʔaywa]	['ʔe:wa]	cloud

[i:] → [e:]
[u:] → [o:]

['di:qa]	['de:wa]	wolf
['si:ma]	['se:ma]	silver
['bi:lan]	['be:lan]	between (us)
['tʰi:la]	['θe:la]; [še:la]	came (she)
[ɹu:]	[ɹo:]	in
[ba'šu:lɪ]	[mba'šo:lɪ]	cooking
[tʰu:p]	[tʰo:p]	rifle

[u] → [ü]

KOINE	SHAMIZDIN	
+[ya'qu:ra]	+[ya'qü:ra]	heavy
['ʔurxa]	['ʔürxa]	way
+['tu:ra]	+['tü:ra]	mountain
['su:sa]	['sü:sa]	horse
['cʰunda]	['cʰünda]	lump of dough

[a] → [i]

KOINE	QUDSHANIS	
['ra:ba]	['ri:ba]	much
[ša'pi:ra]	[ši'pi:ra]	beautiful
[ba'si:ma]	[bi'si:ma]	delicious; thanks
+[ʔa'qɪrwa]	+[ʔi'qarwa]	scorpion
[ša'ma:ša]	[ši'ma:ša]	deacon

[a] → [e]

KOINE	JILU	
[xa:]	[xe:]	one
['ɹa:mi]	['ge:mi]	ship
['ɹa:rɪ]	['ge:rɪ]	roof

$[u] \rightarrow [\text{ɪ} + f]$

KOINE	BAZ	
['ba:bu]	['ba:bɪf]	his father
['yɪmmu]	['yɪmmɪf]	his mother
['be:tʰu]	['bayyɪf]	his house
['xa:tʰu]	['xa:tʰɪf]	his sister

Those are some of the differences in pronunciation that linger in the speech of some individuals or groups as tribal/regional leftovers in the Koine. In the next sections differences in metathesis, emphasis and stress will be dealt with. They are all treated as long features (prosodic) because the change is not confined to one segment only.

2.6.2.2. Metathesis

It is true that metathesis as a marker of difference between the Koine and the tribal dialects is less pervasive than the difference in sound segments. Nonetheless, it is quite striking to the ear of the average speaker of the Koine because, firstly, it involves more than one segment. For instance, it is not unusual for the listener to miss the change in vowel quality or changes resulting from aspiration and spirantization, but the phonetic disorder imposed by metathesis can hardly pass unnoticed. Secondly, metathesis, as a universal phenomenon associated with child language acquisition, is usually received with fun and delight. It is probably due to this psychological fact that metathesis in the speech of adults attracts so much attention. Thirdly, the words that are involved in this type of phonetic change enjoy a high frequency of occurrence and could be treated as part of the core vocabulary of NA.

KOINE	TRIBAL/REGIONAL	
[bɪt] + ['qu:ra]	[bɪq] + ['tu:ra]	cemetery
['ɟni:ɥɪ]	['ɟɥi:nɪ]	eyebrows
+['xa:zɪd]	['sa:xɪd]	to harvest
['xarbɪs]	['xarzɪp]	to push
['xle:pʰa]	['lxe:pʰa]	quilt
+['xma:ta]	+['mxa:ta]	needle
['cʰxa:cʰa]	['xcʰa:cʰa]	laughing
		(initial [cʰ] < [ɟ])

[čʰɪnˈɟɪrra]	[cʰɪnˈǰɪrra][6]	a piece of cloth; rag
[ˈmaǰɟu]	[ˈmaɟǰu]	balloon
[ˈma:cʰɪs]	[ˈmcʰa:sɪ]	to cover
[spaˈdi:tʰa]	[staˈbi:tʰa]	pillow
[ʔaˈqubra]	[ʔaˈbuqra]	mouse
[ˈqa:yɪš]	[ˈʔa:qɪš]	to be cold
+[ˈqa:yɪr]	+[ˈʔa:qɪr]	to dig; peel a coating
+[ˈruxsat]	+[ˈrusxat]	leave; permission
[tʰɪzˈbɪyyɪ]	[tʰubˈzɪyyɪ]	rosary; worry beads

2.6.2.3. Emphasis

It is obvious to any investigator that emphasis is prevalent in all NA dialects, so the concern here is not to demonstrate that the Koine is more or less susceptible to this phonetic phenomenon. The only aspect of emphasis that is of interest here is the fact that the Urmi dialect and the Koine are fairly similar in assigning or denying the features of emphasis to a certain root. In this regard, the Koine is, therefore, unlike the non-Urmi dialects.

KOINE	TRIBAL/REGIONAL	
+[ˈbɪsra]	[ˈbɪsra]	meat
+[ˈɟɪrwɪ]	[ˈɟɪrqɪ]	socks
+[ˈǰaˈna:war]	[ǰaˈna:qar]	monster
+[ˈxalwa]	[ˈxɪlya]	milk
+[yaˈri:xa]	[yaˈri:xa]	tall; long
+[laˈwa:ša]	[laˈwa:ša]	large, flattened, thin bread
+[ˈmɪsta]	[ˈmɪsta]	hair
+[ˈʔayba]	[ˈʔe:ba]	shame
+[ˈʔaywa]	[ˈʔe:wa]	cloud
+[ˈʔayna]	[ˈʔe:na]	eye
+[ˈqɪssa]	[ˈqɪssa]	forehead
+[ˈqɪtʰra]; +[ˈcʰɪtʰra]	[ˈqɪtʰra]	knot

Relevance of emphasis in the following list of words is in the reversed order of the one above.

---

6 A complicated form of metathesis where the palatals and the palato-alveolars are exchanging places and manner of phonation.

KOINE	TRIBAL/REGIONAL	
[ǰuˈqa:la]	+[ǰuˈwa:la]	sack
[čʰaˈpʰu:la]	+[tṣaˈpʰu:la]	slap
[ˈmi:la] blue	+[miˈla:na]	green
[ˈʔaqla]	+[ˈʔaqla]	leg
[ˈʔi:da]	+[ˈʔayda]	feast
[ˈtʰa:pʰi]	+[ˈta:pʰi]	light

2.6.2.4. Stress placement

Stress placement in the Koine and the rest of NA dialects is fairly stable and is predominantly on the penultimate syllable. In all varieties this consistency is occasionally violated. But the violation could be different from one dialect to the other. Therefore, it is quite natural to observe that some of the speakers of the Koine fail to abide by the stress of certain linguistic patterns under the influence of their native dialects. The following are certain deviant patterns from speakers of Baz and Jilu dialects.

KOINE	BAZ	JILU	
[maˈxɪnnɪ]	[ˈma:xɪnnɪ]	[ˈma:xɪnanɪ][7]	I hit him
+[qatˈlɪnnɪ]	[ˈkatlɪnnɪ]	[ˈka:tɪlnanɪ]	I kill him
[šaˈtʰɪnnɪ]	[ˈša:tʰɪnnɪ]	[ˈša:tʰɪnanɪ]	I drink it
+[qarˈtɪnnux]	[ˈkartɪnnux]	[ˈka:rɪtnanux]	I bite you

---

[7] [ˈme:xɪnanɪ] i.e., [a] → [e] is possible in another sub-Jilu dialect.

CHAPTER III

THE CONSONANTAL SYSTEM

3.1. Introductory Remarks

Generally speaking, it is not an easy task to determine which sounds are of phonological significance in various NA dialects because:

(a) They have diverged differently from the old language (if it is ever reasonable to assume that the dialects are all traceable to one form of the old language) because of different patterns in internal change.
(b) They have fallen heavily under the influence of Semitic (Arabic) and non-Semitic (Turkish, Persian, Kurdish) languages. The extent of the influence differs from one dialect to the other.
(c) The descriptive literature dealing with these dialects is very scarce.

The work on the Koine was even more frustrating in the initial stage because:

(a) It has diverged considerably from SWL, Urmi and non-Urmi dialects.
(b) It demonstrates a certain degree of instability due to its recent formation.
(c) The dialect is identified for the first time. This entails the absence of any previous systematic description.

3.2. Theoretical Approaches and Practical Criteria of Investigation

In conducting the analysis of the consonantal system of the Koine, three major linguistic approaches were consulted: Standard Phonemics, Prosodic Analysis (Firth, 1957; Robins, 1970) and Generative Phonology, each being useful and practical in the investigation and description of a certain aspect of the Koine. Standard Phonemics was practical in dealing with the segmental units but it was less so in dealing with the suprasegmental (prosodic) features. This is why the latter aspect was treated in terms of the Firthian approach to phonology. Emphasis, for instance, can hardly be accounted for in phonemic terms without much unwanted complications and inaccuracies. Hence, the Firthian (prosodic) approach replaced the phonemic approach in the treatment of emphasis. Generative Phonology affords a psycholinguistic insight which can fairly accurately assist in determining the phonological status of the units involved through the monitoring of the intuitive responses of the untrained and unsophisticated native speakers to their own sounds. The innate readiness of children for language acquisition and the perfection with which they internalize the bits and pieces (whether as features or segments) and the rules that govern their coordination and production make them grow into the best "sound-tasters." In other words, the response of the native speaker to the sounds of his language should have a great weight in determining their phonological significance i.e., as relevant components in the internalized system. This dimension of Generative Phonology was invoked as an investigatory criterion after an interesting personal experience. As a student I discovered how excellent I was in articulating some complicated aspirated and unaspirated sets of sounds though I was less impressive in articulating sounds involving other feature combinations. When later I embarked on phonological investigation, especially of NA, I discovered the secret to my "excellent performance": I was merely producing sounds that turned out to be most characteristic of the phonology of NA as spoken by the Assyrians.

Within the above theoretical framework the investigation was initiated and the following techniques and criteria were used.

3.2.1. The Commutation Test

It is simply defined as the technique for comparing expressions that, ideally, are alike in all but a single phonetic feature. If such a difference is correlated with a difference in meaning, the phonetic feature is established as functional or phonemic (Dinneen, 1967:36). The units used for this test are known as minimal pairs.

3.2.2. Synchronically Unmotivated Occurrences of Sounds

This procedure attaches significance to the occurrences of sounds which are not contextually conditioned or snychronically motivated. Expressed differently, their occurrence in a certain context is arbitrary. This arbitrariness increases the likelihood of their phonological significance. In fact, this criterion is so significant that even with the neutralization of the role of minimal and near-minimal pairs, it still retains the power to confirm the autonomous functional role of a sound. The significance of this criterion becomes even greater with languages for which minimal pairs are not readily attested.

To shed more light on this technique let us consider the status of the unaspirated sounds in English and the Koine. In English they are primarily restricted to sequences of consonants in which the first element is /s/. Elsewhere, especially in association with stress, they occur as aspirated. Thus one tends to infer that those unaspirated instances are no more than contextually conditioned or synchronically motivated variants of the aspirated sounds. In the Koine the situation will turn out to be rather different partly because the unaspirated sounds occur not only after /s/ but also after the other two fricatives, /š/ and /x/, and partly because unconditioned instances of these sounds are easily attested in all three structural positions. Hence, the unaspirated sounds in English are regarded phonologically insignificant while those in the Koine will be granted phonological significance.

A look at the following lists of words containing the aspirated and unaspirated sounds will clearly indicate their phonological significance in the Koine in initial and medial positions. In final positions they tend to be in free variation due to the optional release of the stop phase of the plosive, a case similar to what a native speaker of English experiences.

[p, t, c, č]		[pʰ, tʰ, cʰ, čʰ]	
+['pa:rɪ]	odd numbers	+['pʰa:rɪ]	lambs
+['pɪllan]	plan	+['pʰɪllan]	so and so (person); our radish
+['paltun]	coat	+['pʰaltun]	(you) get ... out
['patpɪt]	to whisper	['pʰatʰpʰɪt]	to tear apart
+['pla:ša]	fighting	['pʰla:xa][1]	working
+[pa'la:ša]	fighter	[pʰa'la:xa][1]	worker
['partɪc]	slip out of place	['pʰartʰɪx]	to crumble
+[pa'pa:ra]	silly; awkward	+[pʰar'pʰu:rɪ]	blowing (the nose)
+['ʔarpa]	four	+['sarpʰa]	to feel the pungency (f.)
['ʔarpi]	forty	['sarpʰi]	sup up (they)
['ti:na]	because they are	['tʰi:na]	fig
['ti:ɥa]	because he was	['tʰi:ɥa]	sitting
['ti:lɪ]	because he is	['tʰi:lɪ]	he came
['tantɪn]	to hum	['tʰantʰɪn]	to smoke
['tupra]	tail	['tʰupʰxa]	spilled
['tarpɪt]	to make a slight move	['tʰarbɪt]	the fat of
['surta]	small (f)	+['surtʰa]	image

1 The absence of emphasis in these two pieces and others has nothing to do with the presence or absence of aspiration as the two phenomena are the outcome of two physiologically autonomous mechanisms. Aspiration/nonaspiration is essentially a glottal activity whereas emphasis is a supra-glottal activity.

['calla]	unfortunate (m)	['cʰalla]	buffalo
['callɪ]	unfortunate (f)	['cʰallɪ]	buffaloes
['cassi]	religious title	['cʰa:si]	my cup
['carcɪr]	to become deaf	['cʰarcʰɪr]	to giggle
['carra]	deaf	+['cʰarra]	butter
[cur'ti:la]	pup	[cʰur'tʰɪlla]	twisted
['carcɪt]	to tickle	['cʰarcʰuc]	Kirkuk (city)
['čɪnna]	base (in a game)	['čʰanna]; [čʰan'nɪcʰtʰa]	chin
[ča'pultʰa]	hand (dim.)	[čʰa'pu:la]	slap
[čur'čɪrrɪ]	shouted	[čʰɪr'čʰɪrrɪ]	machine gun
[ʔɪčča'bɪčča]	minutia	['čʰɪččʰa]	breast (dim.)
[pač'pu:čɪ]	whispering	['čʰaq'čʰu:qɪ]	chattering
[čan'ču:nɪ]	reverberating	[čʰam'čʰu:mɪ]	flinging
[čɪc'callɪ]	slippers	[čʰɪl'la:lɪ]	rootlets

Crucial to this study is the identification of aspiration/non-aspiration as an important component of the sound system of the Koine. This conclusion is equally pertinent to several other NA dialects, especially those spoken by the Assyrians. In previous literature on NA this phenomenon has not been granted phonological weight. Osipoff (1913), Marogulov (1935) and Polotsky (1961) have reported the phonetic presence of the unaspirated sounds but no systematic phonological judgment was passed. +/t/, the alveolar emphatic and /q/ are also phonetically unaspirated, but their feature of non-aspiration is usually discarded as being phonologically redundant since they are distinguishable on the basis of other features (Odisho et al., 1975).

To report this component of Manner of Phonation as a distinctive feature enhances the accuracy of the synchronic description of the Koine phonology.

3.2.3. Natural Classes of Sounds and Symmetry in System

Natural classes of sounds are those that share maximum common properties and could be described with a minimum number of distinctive features (Fromkin & Rodman, 1983:84). The system of any language is enhanced in symmetry when it displays a greater number of natural classes of sounds. In turn, the phonological symmetry further reinforces the power of other criteria that have already substantiated the phonological significance of sounds as single units. So if it happens that a certain sound fills a slot on any classificatory dimension alongside other sounds then one would consider the process of filling those slots rather systematic than haphazard. For example, in the Koine it has been observed that not only the voiceless aspirated bilabial plosive /pʰ/ has an unaspirated counterpart; /tʰ/, /cʰ/, with which /pʰ/ forms a natural class of voiceless plosives, have also unaspirated counterparts thus leading to a second natural class of unaspirated plosives with no gap in the whole correlation.

3.2.4. Native Speaker's Intuition

Initially one might think that this is not so reliable a criterion as the previous ones because it could involve the subjective response of the native speaker to his language. But when the "subjective" responses recur consistently and with a great number of native speakers, they should no longer be regarded so. In fact, they start gaining more objective weight. This view conforms with the psycholinguistic differences between the processes of first and second languages acquisition. The general observation is that the native speaker (first language learner) tends to have difficulty in perceiving and producing sounds that are not internalized as part of the system. To put it differently a distinctive sound is the one that occupies a true point in the sound pattern and not a mere variant form (Sapir, 1972). In this study the responses obtained from the native speakers of the Koine were quite consistent with the results obtained by applying other systematic procedures. It is, therefore, reasonable to conclude that the success or failure of a statistically significant number of the native speakers of a given language in accurately perceiving and producing a given sound is a highly reliable method for establishing the phonological relevance of that sound.

3.3. *Controversial Sounds and Alphabetic Representation*

An interesting way of looking at the sound system of a language is through its alphabetic characters. Undoubtedly, many would claim that this is an unscientific method that lacks objectivity. Nevertheless, the claim is not supposed to be always true. After all, the alphabetic characters imply an evolutionary sense of depicting the sounds of speech. It so happens that the most recurrent and unmarked sounds are usually granted autonomous symbols. Unmarked sounds are those with higher frequency of occurrence and greater stability in a language. This relationship seems to obtain between the Aramaic alphabetic characters and the most unmarked sounds in NA. Although the sounds /ž, ġ, čʰ, ǰ/ and the unaspirated ones /p, t, c, č/ emerged with phonological relevance in the Koine, most investigators of NA have described the first group as unstable and essentially occurring in loanwords while the phonological status of the second group has hardly been discussed in a systematic way. What is noteworthy in this regard is that all those sounds do not have autonomous symbols to represent them exclusively. /ž, ġ, čʰ, ǰ/ are indicated by diacritical marks added to characters already standing for some of the unmarked sounds while /p, t, c, č/ have no graphic representation. This situation does not seem to be a coincidence; it tends, at least in this case, to imply some phonological significance in that sounds that have an independent graphic representation are more likely to be phonologically relevant.

3.4. *Inventory of the Koine Consonants*

After a thorough application of the approaches and procedures in 3.2. above, the sounds in the chart of Fig. 1 constitute the consonantal system of the Koine.

3.5. *Conventions for the Interpretation of the Chart*

The three basic parameters of consonant description, *Voicing/Voicelessness*, which for convenience is labeled the *Manner of Phonation*, the *Place of Articulation* and the *Manner of Articulation* are used here as in any standard chart in modern phonology. In manner of articulation Ladefoged's (1982) approach to consonant classification is followed with some modification. The phenomena of emphasis and gemination are marked outside the chart to indicate their relevance to all units inside the chart. Further conventions are expounded in detail below to help with the interpretation.

3.5.1. Place of Articulation

This is displayed along the horizontal dimension. The points along this dimension are more restricted than, for instance, in Arabic or English. Compared with the points manipulated in Arabic, the Koine lacks a few major points, namely, labio-dental, inter-dental, velar and pharyngeal. However, the restriction placed on this dimension seems to be compensated for by further elaborations on the manner-of-phonation dimension where three points on the VOT (Voice Onset Time or the synchronization between the glottal and the supraglottal activities) are used in the Koine as opposed to two points for Arabic. This elaboration has yielded six additional sounds that do not exist in Arabic: /pʰ, p, t, c, čʰ, č/.

It is also important to transcribe the last triplet in the set of /pʰ, p, b, tʰ, t, d, cʰ, c, ɟ/ plosives in this form because they are truly palatal not velar. To transcribe them as /kʰ, k, g/, as many scholars usually do, would be quite misleading without

CHART OF CONSONANTS
PLACE OF ARTICULATION

		BILABIAL	ALVEOLAR	PALATO-ALVEOLAR	PALATAL	UVULAR	GLOTTAL
PLOSIVE	VOICED	b	d		ɟ		
	VOICELESS UNASPIRATED	p	t		c	q	ʔ
	VOICELESS ASPIRATED	pʰ	tʰ		cʰ		
AFFRICATE				ǰ č čʰ			
FRICATIVE			z s	ž š		ġ x	h
APPROXIMANT	CENTRAL	ʮ			(ɥ) y		
	LATERAL		l				
	NASAL	m	n				
TAP			r				

MANNER OF ARTICULATION

EMPHASIS

GEMINATION

Fig. 1. Consonantal inventory of the Koine

accurate description of their phonetic nature. The velar triplet does not have any phonological function in the Koine. They are only attested in a very small number of baby-talk vocabulary e.g. [ˈkakka] "anything delicious," [ˈkuːku] or [ˈguːgu] "monster" or in a few of the recently introduced loanwords e.g. [kɪrˈtoːpɪ] "potatoes," +[kʰlaːs] "class," +[glaːs] "glass" (the latter two words are adopted with their British English pronunciation as opposed to their American English pronunciation as [kʰlæs] and [glæs]). In other contexts, both native words and early loanwords, the /kʰ, k, g/ velar triplet is consistently replaced with its palatal counterpart. However, velar plosives could have phonological significance in other NA dialects, viz. Jilu.

3.5.2. Manner of Articulation

Here several points are noteworthy. The first four basic manners of articulation are arranged in terms of the degree of occlusion and the degree of obstruction to the airstream. Plosives represent maximum occlusion (hence maximum obstruction) while approximants represent minimum occlusion. The nature of the occlusion is determined by the degree to which the active and passive articulators are brought together to perform the required obstruction. For demonstration see Fig. 2 below.

In Fig. 2, the straight line represents the passive articulator, which is often immobile, and the bent line represents the active articulator which is most often mobile. When there is a complete contact between the passive and the active articulators and the contact is maintained for a reasonable duration and then terminated with a sudden release the sound is called *plosive* (stop). If the contact is followed by a gradual separation of the articulators the sound is called an *affricate*. If there is no contact but simply a close approximation between the articulators allowing the airstream to force itself through a narrow aperture causing turbulent noise (perceptible friction) the sound is known as a *fricative*. If, however, there is an open approximation resulting in a wide aperture which allows the airstream to flow freely without any friction the sound becomes an *approximant*.[2]

In arranging the approximants in the chart the glides (semivowels), the liquid and the nasals are all included in this category–an approach which is unlike that of Ladefoged. What is common for all approximants is the continuous flow of air through the oral or the nasal passage without turbulent noise. Thus, although a complete oral occlusion is effected for the nasals, the velum is, nevertheless,

---

[2] For details on manner of articulation see Abercrombie (1967), Catford (1977) and Ladefoged (1982).

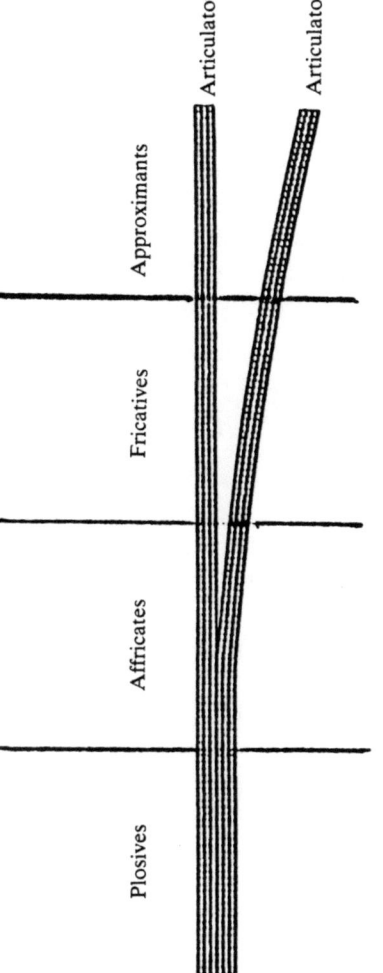

Fig. 2. Schematic representation of the Manner of Articulation of Consonants

lowered and the airstream flows freely through the nasal passage. This entails that the placement of the nasals within the category of approximants is acoustically and auditorily more appropriate than placing them with the plosives or retaining them separate.

The term "tap" has been found necessary for the description of the basic maneuver required for the production of a certain kind of "r" sound common in many languages viz. Aramaic, Arabic, Spanish, Italian etc. A tap [r] is frequently the result of a single and momentary contact between the tongue and the alveolar ridge. If this maneuver is repeated two or more times the sound converts into a *rolled* "r," also called a *trill*. Usually languages that have a tap "r" also have a trilled one.

3.5.3. Manner of Phonation and VOT

The VOT stands for the different ways in which the glottal and supraglottal activities are phonetically synchronized and phonologically manipulated. The Koine utilizes three types of synchronization:
(a) When the glottal activity (voicing) precedes the release of the plosive, the sound is *voiced*.
(b) When voicing is initiated with the release of the plosive, the sound is *voiceless unaspirated*.
(c) When voicing comes after the release of the plosive, the sound is *voiceless aspirated*.

Sounds described in terms of this parameter are arranged vertically beginning with the voiced and ending with the voiceless aspirated. If the three-way classification is missing, the sounds are reduced to a voiced and voiceless dichotomy.

3.5.4. Gemination: Doubling of Consonants

Some languages grant phonological status to geminated consonants. Consequently, they have consonantal oppositions the members of which may be marked as short and long. The Koine uses this phonological device maximally so that every consonantal element undergoes a short/long opposition although the process stipulates syllable restructuring. Krotkoff's observations concerning gemination in the NA dialect of Aradhin seem to be valid for the Koine. In most cases, but not all, gemination seems to compensate for the length of the preceding vowel (Krotkoff, 1982). In the Koine the single consonant is frequently preceded by a long vowel as opposed to a short vowel of its geminated counterpart. Notice the examples below.

SINGLE CONSONANT		GEMINATED CONSONANT	
/cʰuːra/	blind	/cʰurra/	ass
/maːya/	bringing	/mayya/	brings (f.)
/miːtʰa/	dead (m)	/mɪttʰa/	dead (f.)
/saːma/	portion	/samma/	poison
/ʔiːšu/	proper name (Jesus)	/ʔɪššu/	nickname (Elizabeth)
/pʰaːya/	baking	/pʰayya/	bakes (f.)
+/saːwa/	thirst	+/sawwa/	satisfy (thirst or hunger, f.)
/qaːtʰi/	for me	/qattʰi/	my handle
+/tiːna/	clay	+/tɪnna/	carried (f.)
/tʰiːna/	fig	/tʰɪnna/	smoke

Phonetically gemination in plosives and affricates is performed by the prolongation of the stop phase while in fricatives and approximants it is performed by the retention of the whole posture of the sound concerned for a longer period. Due to this fact, the aspiration superscript "h" is not marked on the first element of a geminated aspirated plosive.

3.5.5. Emphasis *(tafxiːm)*

Unlike Arabic, which has four graphically represented emphatics, Aramaic has only two "Ṣādē" and "Ṭēth." In actual performance of the Koine, emphasis is far more widespread both phonetically and phonologically. The [ṭ] for Ṭēth and [ṣ] for Ṣādē do not appear in the chart because:

(a) Emphasis covers almost every segment in the inventory though sounds in the palatal region are less susceptible to emphasis than the labial, alveolar and the uvular. Sounds in the alveolar region are typical in assuming the features of emphasis. This is accounted for in terms of articulatory constraints which will be dealt with in due course. Because of the comprehensive nature of emphasis as a phonological device it is indicated by the large bracket which embraces the whole inventory.

(b) Emphasis is treated as a suprasegmental property or a prosody because its phonetic features are hardly confined to a single segment in the flow of speech; they are often assigned to the syllable or the word. Consequently, the presence of emphasis in the transcription of words is indicated by a "+" in front of the square brackets and the slants.

Although the emphatic /č/ is phonologically transcribed with the same symbol preceded by a "+" sign, its phonetic realization is an unaspirated alveolar affricate [ts̩]. This procedure is adopted for phonological convenience as well as phonetic similarity. For if [ts̩] is treated as an autonomous sound then it will appear as the most isolated unit in the Koine in that it has no direct counterparts whether in terms of voicing or aspiration or emphasis. It is this isolated status of [ts̩] together with the phonetic similarity that it shares with /č/ = [tš] that justify its treatment as the emphatic counterpart of the latter. However, we have to draw the attention to the fact that the only major difference between [ts̩] and [tš] is the place of articulation. The forward shift in the place of articulation may be attributed to the availability of better chances for anchoring the tip of the tongue at the alveolar zone (where [ts̩] is produced) than at the palato-alveolar zone (where [tš] is produced), a condition that is required to counter the tendency to tamper with the primary articulation under the pressure of the rearward movement of the tongue into the pharyngeal cavity–a maneuver which is the most important determinant of the phenomenon of emphasis.

Such a shift in the place of articulation is also noticed with [ɥ] and its emphatic cognate [w] where the palatal location of the former does not seem compatible with the rearward gesture of the tongue. Apparently, the backward drift from the palatal location of [ɥ] into the velar location of [w] brings a better compatibility with emphasis. In an earlier work (Odisho, 1975), the nature of [ɥ] was not satisfactorily identified. It was thought then that the Koine had /w/ as the primary phonological unit with some secondary contextual variants. More lip rounding was reported for one of its variants, but the failure to realize the change in the place of articulation of that variant made the investigation fall short of identifying it as [ɥ]. Further investigation since then has firmly established [ɥ] as a characteristic sound in the Koine. From the phonological point-of-view, it is obvious that [ɥ] and [w] are in complementary distribution since the occurrence of [w] is confined to emphatic contexts and before back vowels. Another phonological revision relevant in this respect is the treatment of /ɥ/ as the underlying (abstract) form from which [w] is derived. The rationale for this treatment stems from the fact that when the native speakers of the Koine embark on learning foreign languages, the dominant trend is to replace the [w] and [v] (Koine has no [v]) in those languages with [ɥ]. They usually experience great difficulty in mastering [w] and [v].

Most interesting in this regard is that the very existence of [ɥ] in the system is apparently tied up with the presence of the palatal triplet [c^h, c, ɟ] rather than the velar triplet [k^h, k, g]. In other words, [ɥ] as a palatal is more compatible with the palatal category; in fact from the articulatory point-of-view, it is very difficult to combine [ɥ] in the form of clusters with any member of the velar sounds.

CHAPTER IV

THE VOWEL SYSTEM

4.1. *Introductory Remarks*

The basic vowel system in the Semitic languages is a triangular one i.e.,

```
    i     u
       a
```

This system is still valid for Standard Arabic. However, historical changes have expanded the three-vowel system into a primarily five-vowel system which is attested in many dialects of Arabic. The additional two vowel qualities that have emerged are /e/ and /o/, thus yielding the following pattern:

```
    i     u
    e     o
       a
```

A similar system is characteristic of NA in general, though different varieties of NA manifest minor differences both in quality and quantity.

4.2. *Methods of Investigation*

Investigation is conducted in terms of the structural positions of vowels and the syllable and word structures in which the vowels occur. The structural position of vowels involves a survey of all the occurrences of vowel qualities in medial and final positions.[1] The syllable and word structure involves the examination of open and closed syllables. Abercrombie's (1967) definition of the terms "open" and "closed" is followed. According to Abercrombie, a syllable which is arrested by a consonant is said to be closed, and one which has no arresting consonant is said to be open. A further elaboration is added when the "syllable pattern" is considered. The syllable pattern is used to specify the number of the consonants in each position as well as the quality and the quantity of the vowels involved. The aim of

---

1 Vowels do not occur in initial position.

this examination, which is made in the context of monosyllabic and polysyllabic words, is to determine the distributional behavior of each vowel and whether there are any gaps in their occurrence. Both facts are of paramount significance in establishing the phonological status of a given vowel.

Using the symbols "C", "V" and "0" to stand for a consonant, vowel and zero segments respectively, all the instances of vowel occurrence can be exhaustively expressed. Vowel quantity (length) is identified as short or long and is indicated by the presence or absence of a colon i.e., (:) after the vowel, a convention that is so common in phonetic transcription. It should be pointed out, however, that a narrower representation of vowel quantity in the Koine will grant certain vowels a half length.[2] But since such an elaboration has never been reported to have any phonological weight in any language, therefore, any consideration of it here will be vacuous. Half length will be marked only when comparative phonetics is involved.

4.3. *Syllable Structures and Patterns in Polysyllabic Words*

In this section all the possible syllable structures and patterns of the Koine will be surveyed in the contexts of polysyllabic words. The relevant syllables are underlined.

4.3.1. CV0 Syllables

(a) CV0 IN INITIAL POSITION

		VOWEL QUALITY
[si'me:lɪ]	he has ordained them	[i]
[bɪ'tʰa:ya]	coming	[ɪ]
[be'tʰe:]	their house	[e]
[na'xi:ra]	nose	[a]
[ho'na:na]	clever	[o]
[su'ra:ya]	Assyrian	[u]

(b) CV0 IN MEDIAL POSITION

['si:milɪ]	he has ordained me	[i]
['mɪxyelɪ]	he has beaten	[e]
[baba'ɥa:tʰan]	our fathers	[a]

---

[2] Notice the three vowel lengths: ['pʰa:tʰa] "face," [pʰa.'tʰe:] "their face" and [pʰatʰɥa.'tʰe:] "their faces."

[ˈtʰiːloxun]	you came	[o]
[suˈruːtʰa]	childhood; littleness	[u]

(c) CVO IN FINAL POSITION

[ˈnaːši]	my men; my relatives	[i]
[ˈnaːšɪ]	men	[ɪ]
[naˈšeː]	their relative	[e]
[ˈnaːša]	man	[a]
[ˈnaːšo]	her relative	[o]
[ˈnaːšu]	his relative	[u]

4.3.2. C²V0 Syllables³

C₂V0 IN INITIAL POSITION

[msiˈtʰeːla]	she has washed them	[i]
[dreˈtʰeː]	their throw	[e]
[ˈpʰtʰaxena]	they are opening	[a]
[ɹnoˈtʰeː]	their stealing	[o]
[ˈcʰtʰuːtʰa]	writing	[u]

4.3.3. CVC Syllables

(a) CVC IN INITIAL POSITION

[ˈcʰɪrya]	short	[ɪ]
[ˈbaxta]	woman; wife	[a]
[ˈʔordaɹ]	duck	[o]
[ˈsurta]	small (f.)	[u]

(b) CVC IN MEDIAL POSITION

[musˈrɪqli]	I had it combed	[ɪ]
[munˈšiːtʰenɥa]	I had forgotten (f.)	[e]
[cʰaˈnašta]	sweeper (f.)	[a]
[cʰaˈnušta]	broom	[u]

(c) CVC IN FINAL POSITION

[ˈmašrɪq]	to whistle	[ɪ]
[ˈšitʰaˈʔiːtʰ]	annually	[i]
[mušˈrɪqtʰen]	I have whistled (f.)	[e]

---

3 This syllable pattern is attested only in initial position due to the restrictions on the structural position of consonant clusters.

[ˈpʰarxax]	we fly	[a]
[ˈqaːtʰux]	for you	[u]

4.3.4. C²VC Syllable (restricted to initial position)

[ˈcʰništa]	being swept	[ɪ]
[ˈcʰrapʰtʰa]	state of being angry	[a]
[ˈpʰtʰuxta]	spacious (f.)	[u]

4.4. *Syllable Structures and Patterns in Monosyllabic Words*

In this section all the possible syllable structures and patterns of the Koine will be surveyed in the context of monosyllabic words. Due to the nature of NA as a Semitic language, monosyllabic words are rare. This fact imposes strict constraints on the range of syllable structures and their patterns.

4.4.1. CV0 Syllables

		VOWEL QUALITY
[bɪ][4]	the family of	[ɪ]
[siː]	go!	[i]
[heː]	yes!	[e]
[xaː]	one	[a]
[ʔoː]	that	[o]
[quː]	get up!	[u]

4.4.2. C²V0 Syllables

[driː]	pour; throw!	[i]
[tʰreː]	two	[e]
[dlaː]	without	[a]
[ɟnuː]	steal!	[u]

---

[4] It is the reduced form of "bet" meaning "the family of" e.g. [bɪ maˈmuːni] (the family of my uncle).

4.4.3. CVC Syllables

[cʰɪs]	with; beside; near to	[ɪ]
[betʰ]⁵	the house/family of	[e]
[hal]	give!	[a]
[šuq]	leave!	[u]

4.5. *Some Less Common Syllable Structures and Patterns*

Most of the words that contain these less common syllable structures and patterns are imperatives, prepositions, letter names and loan words that are not Aramaicized.

4.5.1. C²VC

		VOWEL QUALITY
[brɪš]	on	[ɪ]
[pʰruq]	finish!	[u]
[šraq traq]	straightforward	[a] This vowel is confined mainly to onomatopoetic words

4.5.2. CVVC or CV:C

[bi:tʰ]	letter name "b"	[i]
[ze:n]	letter name "z"	[e]
[qo:pʰ]	letter name "q"	[o] (also [ɟo:l] "pond"; [čʰo:l] "wilderness." Both are loanwords)
[yu:d]	letter name "y"	[u]
[cʰa:p]	letter name "cʰ"	[a]

4.5.3. CVCC Syllables (loanwords only)

[jɪns]	good	[ɪ]
[marč]	bet	[a]

---

5 Is used in compound words viz., [bet ɟnu:na] (bride-chamber) and in surnames viz., [betˈšli:mun].

4.6. *Further Distributional Examination and Concluding Remarks*

The following minimal and near-minimal pairs also contribute in shedding more light on the distinctive value of the vowels occurring in the Koine.

		VOWEL QUALITY
['mi:tʰa]	dead (m.)	[i]
['mɪttʰa]	dead (f.)	[ɪ] (near minimal pair)
['me:tʰa]	(will) die (f.)	[e]
['mo:tʰa]	death	[o]
['ma:tʰa]	village	[a]

Those five minimal and near-minimal pairs yield five vowel oppositions; but if the following pairs are added another relevant vowel quality will emerge in the medial position.

		VOWEL QUALITY
['ši:ra]	paint	[i]
['še:ra]	verse	[e]
['šo:ra]	(will) jump (f.)	[o]
['šu:ra]	fence	[u]
['ša:na]	hive	[a] (near minimal pair)

The following pairs and near-minimal pairs show six vowel qualities in the final position.

		VOWEL QUALITY
['na:ši]	my men	[i]
['na:šɪ]	men	[ɪ]
[na'še:]	their men	[e] (near minimal pair)
['na:ša]	man	[a]
['na:šo]	her men	[o]
['na:šu]	his men	[u]

The above commutation of vowels tends to suggest that only six vowel qualities enjoy phonological status in the Koine. This is highly consistent with the vowel qualities that recurred in the survey of syllable structures and patterns. Despite the scarcity of certain syllable structures and patterns or the absence of minimal pairs in certain cases, the synchronically unmotivated occurrence of the following six vowels /i, ɪ, a, e, o, u/ establishes their phonological status in the Koine beyond any doubt. Impressionistically placed on a vowel chart the six vowels will occupy the following locations, Fig. 3.

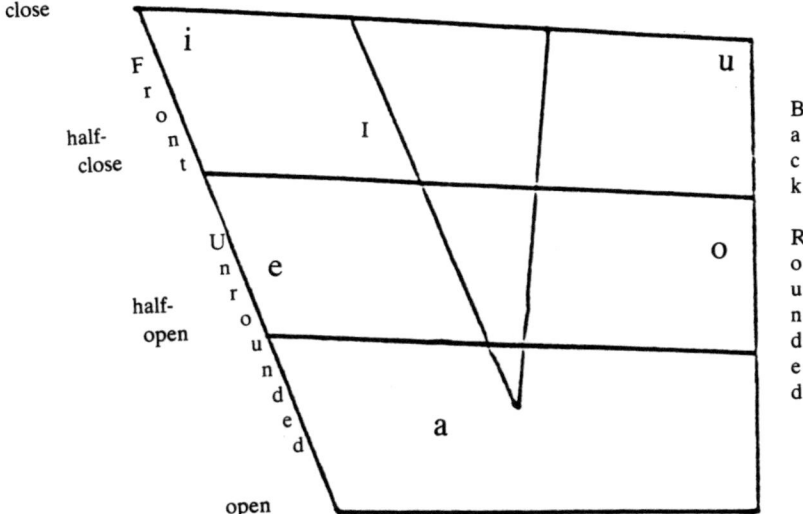

Fig. 3. An impressionistic plotting of Vowels in the Koine.

4.7. Some Salient Characteristics of the Vowel System

Although phonetically vowels in the Koine have three quantitative variants: short, medium (longish) and long, quantity is phonologically irrelevant; hence the length mark is deleted. Full length is usually associated with stress which is predominantly penultimate. This obviously does not exclude the occurrence of short vowels in stressed syllables or longish vowels in unstressed syllables. The former instances are often associated with closed syllable whereas the latter are associated with open syllables in non-final positions. Compared with Urmi, the longish vowels in open unstressed syllables of the Koine show a tendency towards shortening. The word "beautiful" in Urmi is pronounced [ša.ˈpiːra] while in the Koine the following two alternative pronunciations: [ša.ˈpiːra] or [šaˈpiːra] are attested, though the latter is more common.

/ɪ/ cannot have a long variant despite the stress or the openness of the syllable. Other than in final position, the occurrence of /ɪ/ in open syllables is very limited. The short variant of /e/ is very rare finally. Vowel quality range in open syllables is broader than in closed syllables. In fact, in monosyllabic words, other than some marginal words, the range of quality in closed syllable is reduced to three vowels namely, /ɪ, a, u/.

All vowels are subject to emphasis, therefore, their number should phonologically be doubled if emphasis were to be treated phonemically. But since this approach has not been followed, the features of emphasis are, thus, assigned to a longer unit, usually a word. In the context of a word both vowels and consonants are equally susceptible to the phonetic features of emphasis. Vowels in emphatic contexts usually acquire the features of lowness and backness. (For details see Chap. IX.)

4.8. Similar Trend of Change in the Koine and in Urmi

It has already been indicated earlier on that the Koine developed as an offshoot of SWL and that SWL was mainly based on Urmi. Consequently, it is of little surprise to find that the vowel system in the Koine follows a line of divergence from the old language and the non-Urmi dialects similar to that of Urmi. The divergence is highly systematic, especially from the Ashiret dialects. Frequently, the diphthongs /ay/, /aʉ(w)/ change into long /e/, /o/ vowels, respectively. Simultaneously, the latter pair shows a tendency to move into a more close position i.e., /i/, /u/, respectively. Notice the following examples:

(a) /ay/ → /e/
     /aw/ → /o/

BAZ	KOINE & URMI	
/cʰayma/	/cʰema/	be black
+/sayda/	+/seda/	hunting
/saypʰa/	/sepʰa/	sword
+/qayta/	+/qeta/; +/keta/	summer
+/tayra/	+/tera/	bird

TIARI	KOINE & URMI	
+/ɟawra/; +/ǰawra/	+/ɟora/	husband
/cʰawsa/	/cʰosa/	hair
+/qawra/	+/qora/	grave
/šawpʰa/	/šopʰa/	place
/tʰawra/	/tʰora/	ox

The direction of the change is illustrated in the diagram below, Fig. 4.

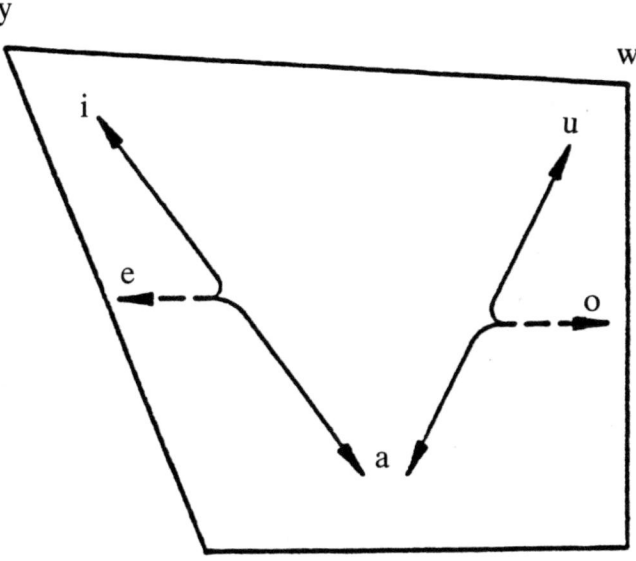

Fig. 4. Vowel diagram showing the contraction of the diphthongs /ay/ and /aq(w)/ into the monophthongs /e/ and /o/, respectively.

(b) /e/ → /i/
     /o/ → /u/

TIARI	KOINE & URMI	
/bena/	/bina/	breath
/dewa/	/diqa/	wolf
/čʰepʰa/	/cʰipʰa/	stone
/sema/	/sima/	silver
/šetʰa/	/šitʰa/	year
/ɟoma/	/ɟuma/	animal shed
/yoma/	/yuma/	day
/ʔaxona/	/ʔaxuna/	brother
+/qatola/	+/qatula/	murderer

The direction of the change is illustrated in the diagram below, Fig. 5.

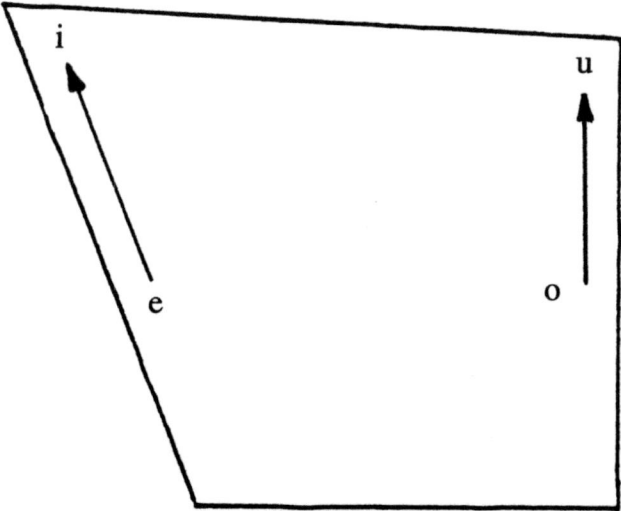

Fig. 5. Vowel diagram showing the shift of /e/ and /o/ into /i/ and /u/, respectively.

The monophthongization tendency in Fig. 4 is the result of a contraction between the two components of the diphthongs. The ends of each solid arrow in Fig. 4 represent the locations of the two components. /y/ and /w/ are marked outside the periphery of the vowel diagram on the assumption that they are of consonantal nature and cannot be placed within the diagram but at the same time they glide from the same positions of /i/ and /u/ cardinal vowels, respectively. The contraction between the two elements of the diphthong leads in each case to a vowel quality that is exactly between the /a/ ⟷ /i/ and /a/ ⟷ /u/ dimensions. It is in this manner that most of the instances of /e/ and /o/ emerge in the Koine and in Urmi.

The elevation of /e/, /o/ vowels to be realized as /i/, /u/ is closely associated with the previous change because this change seems to be evacuating the place for the new instances of /e/ and /o/ that result from the contraction. So the dynamic relationship within the system is unmistakable. If the two changes are collapsed in one diagram the dynamic relationship in the movement of the vocalic elements will look even more convincing (Fig. 6).

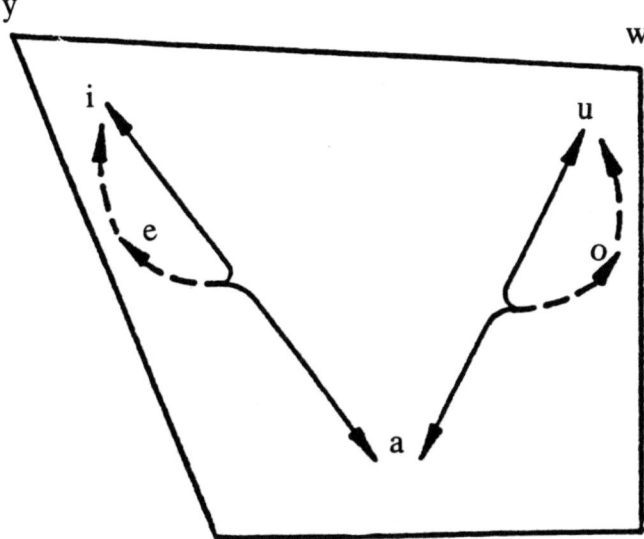

Fig. 6. Vowel diagram combining the vocalic shifts in Figs. 4 and 5 and indicating the systematicness of the shift.

CHAPTER V

CONSONANT CLUSTERS

5.1. Introductory Remarks

This topic is being relatively devoted more space than other topics partly because it is an aspect of NA phonology that has received very little attention, if any, in the recent literature and partly because the phonetic structure of some of the clusters is fairly uncommon in other languages of the world thus making them of interest to general phonetics as well as phonology.

It is important at the outset to explicitly clarify the meaning of "consonant cluster" which has been interpreted differently by different investigators whether in its application to NA or to other languages. In this study, the term is used to denote a sequence of more than one consonant which is restricted to one syllable or as Abercrombie puts it: a sequence that does not extend over two syllables; if the sequence spreads over two syllables then it is no longer a cluster, but rather a sequence of abutting consonants (Abercrombie, 1967:76). So following the above definition, the term is used to exclude abutting consonants. To illustrate, the sequence "tr" in "hatrack" represents abutting consonants while in "contract" it represents a cluster.

This exclusive definition has many implications. Firstly, a cluster can be treated as an entity that can receive stress as a whole unit, whereas in the case of abutting consonants, prominence falls on a certain element(s) of the sequence rather than on the sequence as a whole. This differentiation is relevant to the phonetic realization of the segments involved. For instance, it is more likely for "r" in "contract" to be devoiced than "r" in "hatrack." Secondly, inasmuch as second/foreign language acquisition is concerned, it is the admissible clusters in the target language rather than what is equivalent to them in terms of abutting consonants that pose a serious pronunciation difficulty to the learner. Thirdly, any confusion between consonant clusters and abutting consonants in the sense of treating them as being structurally and phonologically identical, will lead to a drastic difference in the phonological description of a given language. The difference will be reflected mainly in the size of the admissible clusters as well as their structural positions. (For details see Odisho, 1979a.) As for the last point, it has been found that because Al-Ani (1970) applies the term in a loose sense to include abutting consonants, he concludes that Classical Arabic has medial clusters. This is an inaccurate statement because Classical Arabic has no medial clusters. For NA, in this case it is the dialect of Urmi, Hetzron (1969) also concludes that Urmi has medial clusters. This conclusion of Hetzron stems from the same confusion to which Al-Ani had succumbed. So the additional structural place viz., the medial position for clusters in CA and NA, is a fiction brought about by misinterpreting the meaning of cluster.

5.2. *Size of Clusters*

In order to determine the size of the clusters the difference between a *stem* (the radicals of the root and the vowels required to join them) and a *word* (the stem with the affixes) is taken into consideration.

After a thorough survey of the permissible clusters in the Koine, it is concluded that the maximum number of elements in a stem-cluster is two and it increases to three in a word-cluster. For example, clusters such as /pʰtʰ/ in /pʰtʰaxa/ "opening," /šq/ in /šqala/ "taking," +/qt/ in +/qtala/ "killing" and /dq̇/ in /dq̇aqa/ "catching" are to be denoted as stem clusters because both of their components are radicals in the following roots: /pʰtʰx/, /šql/, +/qtl/ and /dq̇q̇/, respectively. Clusters like /db/ in /dbabi/ "my father's" and /lxm/ in /lxmara/ "on the donkey" are word-clusters because the first element in each of them represents a morpheme or a reduced morpheme that is prefixed to the stem. It is obvious that the former word originally begins with one consonant to which another one is prefixed while in the latter, the word originally begins with a cluster of two elements.

5.3. *Structural Location of Clusters*

As for the structural location of clusters, they are almost exclusively restricted to initial positions except for a few loanwords such as /mašq/ "drilling; practice," /marč/ "bet," /janj/ "rust" and /jɪns/ "good." The existence of a few clusters in final position does not constitute a considerable inconsistency in the phonology of the Koine mainly because those words have either a more Aramaicized version which helps dispense with the final cluster e.g., /mašqɪ/ and /janja/ or they are gradually being replaced by native words such as +/ʔɪjra/ for /marč/ and +/spa:y/ for /jɪns/.

To recapitulate, clusters in the Koine occur only initially and are of only two elements in a stem and of three in a word.

5.4. *Types of Clusters*

In this section all the attested clusters are identified in charts. Their phonetic nature and the articulatory constraints that govern their formation are investigated. The main emphasis is on the stem-clusters in both emphatic and unemphatic contexts.

The charts in Figs. 7, 8, display all the existing stem clusters. The consonantal units are arranged according to their manner of articulation i.e., plosives, affricates, fricatives etc. The units on the vertical dimension represent the first element of the cluster while those on the horizontal dimension represent the second element. The existing clusters are indicated by a plus sign. The blank space indicates the absence of the cluster either because it is non-existent or because instances of them have not been, hitherto, attested. The sign "o" attached to a cluster stands either for the likelihood of an alternative pronunciation or that further experimental investigation is needed to substantiate the relevance of certain phonetic features.

5.5. *Concluding Remarks*

Although there tend to be strict constraints on the size and structural positions of clusters in the Koine, it could still show relative richness in the occurrence of clusters. Of particular interest are the double-plosive clusters which are of rare appearance in languages. It is specifically the absence of clusters in final position that poses a serious problem for Assyrians in second language learning. Usually, they break those clusters with epenthetic vowels.

Looking at the charts, one can easily observe a great number of empty spaces which represent the inadmissible clusters. These gaps must either arise from particular constraints or are mere accidental gaps. No doubt, it is difficult to draw a demarcation line between what arises from a constraint and what is an accidental gap. But if the major constraints are specified, then the problem of determining the accidental gaps will become relatively easier.

Speaking in terms of the place of articulation there seems to be a strong tendency not to allow sounds of the same or neighboring place of articulation to combine into clusters. This, probably, accounts for many of the blank spaces that form a large empty band running diagonally from the top left corner of the two charts down to the bottom right corner. Maximum blankness, however, exists in the center. The constraints of place of articulation become less strict when there are differences in the supraglottal manner of articulation; the greater the difference in the manner of articulation the less the strictness arising from the place of

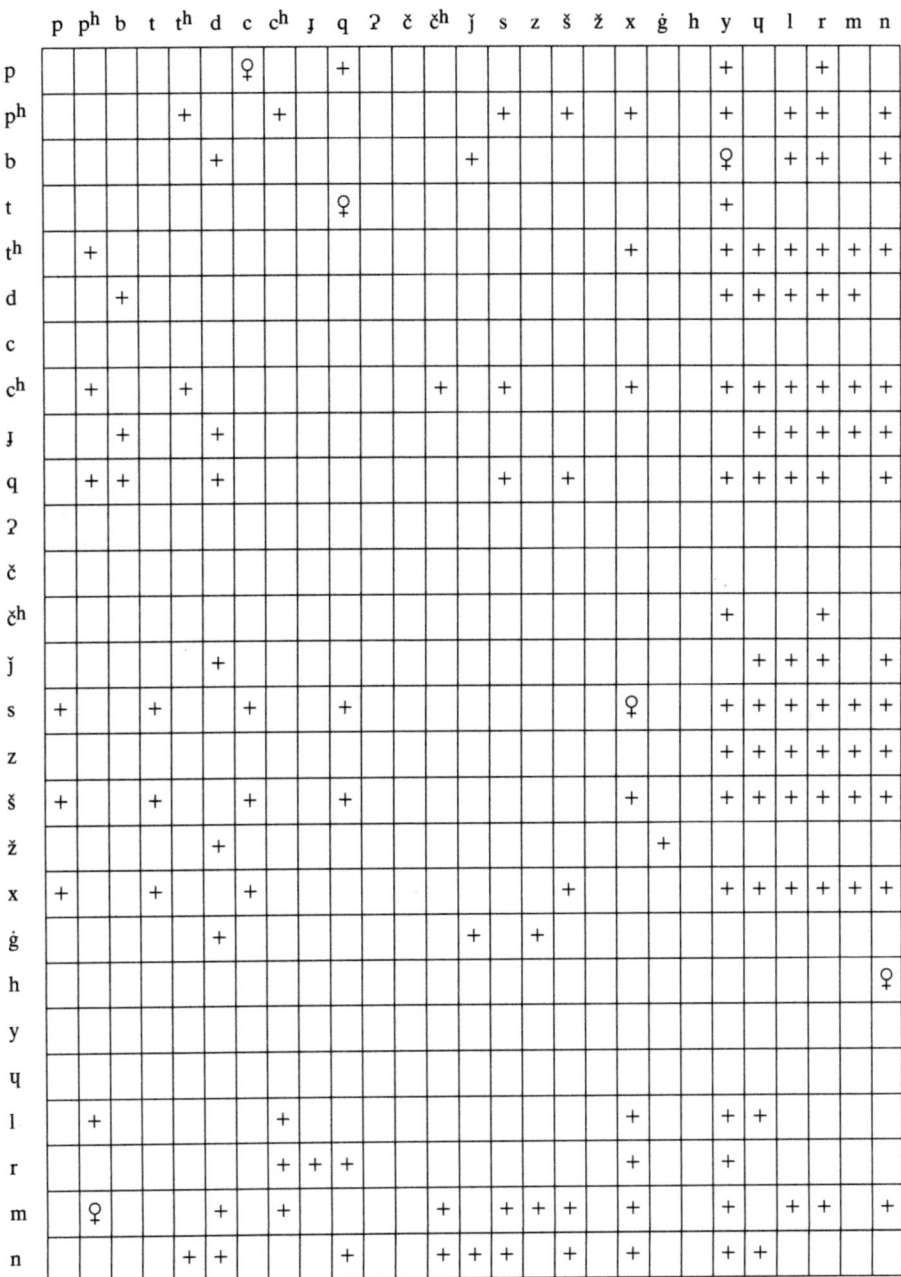

Fig. 7. Chart showing the attested unemphatic stem-clusters in the Koine. Sounds on the vertical dimension form the first element of the cluster.

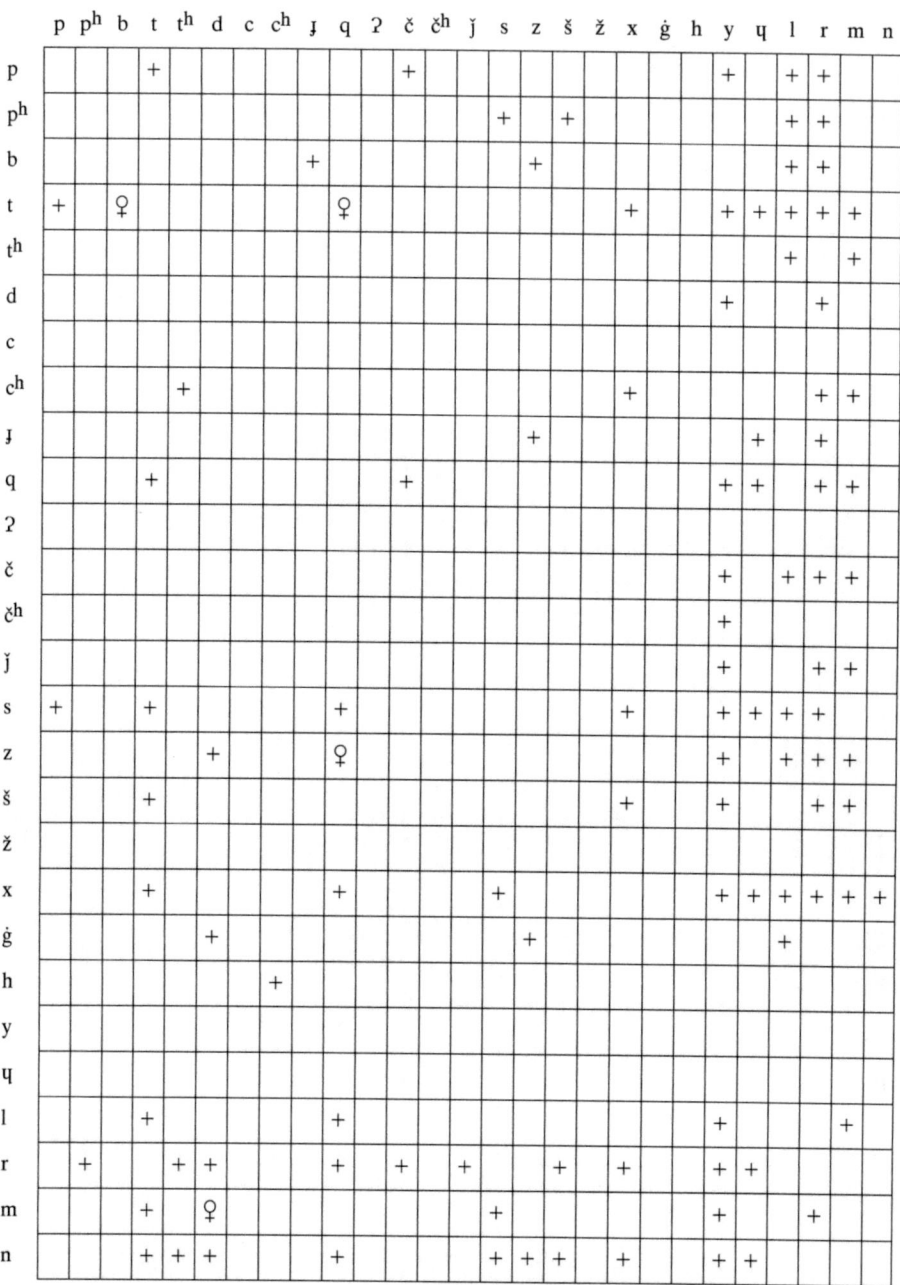

Fig. 8. Chart showing the attested emphatic stem-clusters in the Koine. Sounds on the vertical dimension form the first element of the cluster.

articulation. This partly accounts for the density in the top two-thirds of the right hand side and the bottom four rows of the charts. It is in these areas where the sounds described as approximants form clusters with non-approximants, i.e., the plosives, fricatives and affricates.

Other important constraints, which also seem to function highly consistently, are those related to the behavior of the glottis, described earlier on as the manner of phonation yielding the voiced vs. voiceless and aspirated vs. unaspirated contrasts. The distinctive feature of the first contrast is labelled "glottal activity" and that of the second is labelled "glottal aperture." Here also the combination of sounds involving those two features depends on the extent of the difference between them. The constraints become less effective with the increase in the difference. A considerable number of the blank spaces are the direct outcome of those constraints. In fact, except for a few combinations, the constraints are quite stringent among the non-approximants. Clusters with a combination of voiced and voiceless or aspirated and unaspirated plosives are rarely encountered. The only combinations that are admissible, though not frequently recurrent, may be in the form of a voiceless unaspirated plosive with a voiced one (/qd/ as in /qdala/ "neck") or a voiceless unaspirated plosive with a voiceless aspirated (+/qt^h/ as in +/qt^{h}ara/[1] "making a knot") but never a voiced plosive with a voiceless aspirated one.

Most of the above constraints are universal in that they are valid for most languages. There are also language-specific constraints that are attributed mainly to the absence or rarity of certain sounds in a given language. However, when certain sounds are neither absent nor rare and there are no constraints on their combinations, the absence of clusters involving them is regarded as an accidental gap.

5.6. Lists of Stems Containing the Attested Unemphatic Clusters

CLUSTER	EXAMPLE	MEANING	NOTES
		/p/	
/pc/°	/pcaxa/	blossoming	This is in free variation with /p^{h}c^h/
/pq/	/pqaya/	exploding	

---

[1] This is also realized as +/c^{h}t^{h}ara/.

Consonant Clusters

/py/	/pyača/	"a gesture with the hand indicating insult"	
/pr/	/primus/	paraffin cooker	

/pʰ/

/pʰtʰ/	/pʰtʰaxa/	opening	
/pʰcʰ/	/pʰcʰaya/	losing taste	
/pʰs/	/pʰsama/	recovering	
/pʰš/	/pʰšara/	melting	
/pʰx/	/pʰxaya/	weeping	
/pʰy/	/pʰyaša/	remaining	
/pʰl/	/pʰlaxa/	working	
/pʰr/	/pʰrama/	cutting	
/pʰn/	/pʰnaya/	perishing	

/b/

/bd/	/bdaya/	breaking a promise	
/bǰ/	/bǰara/	growing (int.)	
/by/°	/byaqa/	giving	Although the "b" represents a prefix, the native speaker hardly suspects that it is not part of the root.
/br/	/braya/	taking place or coming into existence	
/bn/	/bnaya/	building	

/t/

/tq/°	/tqala/	weighing	This is in free variation with /tʰq/
/ty/	/tyaraya/	a member of Tiari tribe	

/tʰ/

/tʰpʰ/	/tʰpʰana/	becoming mouldy
/tx/	/txara/	remembering
/tʰy/	/tʰyaqa/	sitting
/tʰq/	/tʰqana/	becoming numb
/tʰl/	/tʰlaya/	hanging

/tʰr/	/tʰraya/	becoming wet
/tʰm/	/tʰmanya/	eight
/tʰn/	/tʰnaya/	repeating

/d/

/db/	/dbaša/	sticking
/dy/	/dyala/	giving birth to
/dʉ/	/dʉaqa/	catching
/dl/	/dlapʰa/	dripping
/dr/	/draya/	throwing or pouring
/dm/	/dmaxa/	sleeping

NB. No clusters with /c/ as the first element.

/cʰ/

/cʰpʰ/	/cʰpʰana/	becoming hungry
/cʰtʰ/	/cʰtʰaʉa/	book or writing
/cʰčʰ/	/cʰčʰaxa/	becoming tired
/cʰs/	/cʰsaxa/	pruning
/cʰx/	/cʰxacʰa/	laughing (initial /cʰ/ is originally /ɉ/)
/cʰy/	/cʰyapʰa/	bending or becoming lower in level
/cʰʉ/	/cʰʉaya/	searing
/cʰl/	/cʰlaya/	standing or waiting
/cʰr/	/cʰraba/	becoming angry
/cʰm/	/cʰma/	how much or how many
/cʰn/	/cʰnaša/	sweeping

/ɉ/

/ɉb/	/ɉbaya/	boiling over
/ɉd/	/ɉdala/	thread
/ɉʉ/	/ɉʉaya/	begging
/ɉl/	/ɉlaya/	uncovering
/ɉr/	/ɉrasa/	grinding
/ɉm/	/ɉmara/	shrinking e.g., cloth
/ɉn/	/ɉnaʉa/	stealing

/q/

/qpʰ/	/qpʰaya/	grabbing or clutching

/qb/	/qbala/	accepting
/qd/	/qdala/	neck
/qs/	/qsaya/	breaking up
/qš/	/qšaya/	becoming thicker or denser
/qy/	/qyada/	burning
/qʠ/	/qʠaya/	emptying water or any fluid from a container or ditch, using a bowl or vessel
/ql/	/qlaya/	frying
/qr/	/qraʠa/	receiving the holy communion
/qn/	/qnaya/	gaining

NB. No clusters with /ʔ/ as the first element.
No clusters with /č/ as the first element.

/čʰ/

/čʰy/	/čʰyada/	inviting
/čʰr/	/čʰrata/	slipping out of place or going off; escaping

/ǰ/

/ǰd/	/ǰdaqa/	tearing apart
/ǰʠ/	/ǰʠaǰa/	moving
/ǰl/	/ǰlaxa/	peeling off the skin or bark as a result of scratching; grazing
/ǰr/	/ǰrapʰa/	slipping
/ǰn/	/ǰnaʠa/	kidnapping[2]

/s/

/sp/	/spaqa/	becoming empty
/st/	/stara/	undoing e.g., knitting
/sc/	/scɪntʰa/	knife

[2] It is a palatalized form of /ɟnaʠa/ "stealing." The two versions trigger a semantic difference (cf. Tsereteli, 1978:33).

Lists of Stems Containing the Attested Unemphatic Clusters

/sq/	/sqada/	losing interest	
/sx/°	/sxada/	worshipping	This is in free variation with /zġ/
/sy/	/syaꭐa/	becoming old	
/sꭐ/	/sꭐadaya/	name for the vernacular variant of Aramaic which is now an acceptable term denoting N.A. both written and spoken	
/sl/	/slaba/	looting	
/sr/	/sraqa/	combing	
/sm/	/smaqa/	becoming red	
/sn/	/snaya/	hating	

/z/

/zy/	/zyara/	swelling
/zꭐ/	/zꭐana/	buying
/zl/	/zlaya/	fracturing
/zr/	/zraqa/	rising e.g., sun
/zm/	/zmara/	singing
/zn/	/znaya/	fornicating

/š/

/šp/	/špala/	paralyzing
/št/	/štaya/	drinking
/šc/	/šcaya/	complaining
/šq/	/šqala/	taking
/šx/	/šxana/	becoming hot
/šy/	/šyapʰa/	erasing; wearing off
/šꭐ/	/šꭐaꭐa/	neighbor
/šl/	/šlaxa/	taking off
/šr/	/šraya/	unfastening
/šm/	/šmayya/	sky
/šn/°	/šnaya/	fainting

/ž/

/žd/	/ždaya/	teasing e.g., cotton
/žġ/	/žġaša/	becoming disturbed e.g., mentally

		/x/	
/xp/	/xpara/		digging
/xt/	/xtama/		finishing
/xc/	/xcama/		governing
/xš/	/xšala/		pounding
/xy/	/xyapʰa/		having a bath
/xʮ/	/xʮaša/		containing
/xl/	/xlepʰa/		quilt
/xr/	/xraʮa/		becoming rotten; going out of order
/xm/	/xmara/		donkey
/xn/	/xnaqa/		strangling

		/ġ/	
/ġd/	/ġdaya/		feeling happy
/ġǰ/	/ġǰala/		feeling amazed, becoming startled
/ġz/	/ġzaya/		seeing

		/h/	
/hn/	/hnaya/		feeling pleased	/nh/ is also possible by metathesis

NB. No clusters with /y/ as the first element.
No clusters with /ʮ/ as the first element.

		/l/	
/lpʰ/	/lpʰaya/		eating greedily
/lcʰ/	/lcʰaxa/		licking
/lx/	/lxama/		fitting
/ly/	/lyaya/		singing mournfully over a dead person
/lʮ/	/lʮaša/		wearing

		/r/	
/rcʰ/	/rcʰaxa/		becoming soft
/rʝ/	/rʝada/		shaking; shivering
/rq/	/rqada/		dancing
/rx/	/rxaqa/		becoming far
/ry/	/ryaqa/		spitting

Lists of Stems Containing the Attested Emphatic Clusters

/m/

/mpʰ/°	/mpʰala/	falling	This is in free variation with /npʰ/
/md/	/mditʰa/	city	
/mcʰ/	/mcʰaxa/	becoming meek	
/mčʰ/	/mčʰaxa/	being available	
/ms/	/msaya/	washing e.g., clothes	
/mz/	/mzida/	a leather bag	
/mš/	/mšixa/	Christ	
/mx/	/mxaya/	beating	
/my/	/myatʰa/	dying	
/ml/	/mlaya/	filling	
/mr/	/mretʰa/	moth	
/mn/	/mnaxa/	The late	

/n/

/ntʰ/	/ntʰara/	taking by force
/nd/	/ndaya/	hopping
/nq/	/nqaza/	hitting the target
/nčʰ/	/nčʰala/	plucking
/nǰ/	/nǰaʠa/	rebuking
/ns/	/nsara/	sawing
/nš/	/nšaqa/	kissing
/nx/	/nxapʰa/	feeling shy
/ny/	/nyaxa/	becoming relieved; dying (fig.)
/nʠ/	/nʠaxa/	barking

5.7. Lists of Stems Containing the Attested Emphatic Clusters

CLUSTER	EXAMPLE	MEANING	NOTES
		/p/	
+/pt/	+/ptaxa/	becoming flat	
+/pč/	+/pčala/	bending, becoming crooked	
+/py/	+/pyaǰa/	feeling depressed or uneasy	
+/pl/	+/plaša/	fighting	

+/pr/	+/prama/	understanding

/pʰ/

+/pʰs/	+/pʰsaxa/	feeling happy
+/pʰš/	+/pʰšama/	feeling sorry
+/pʰl/	+/pʰlata/	going out
+/pʰr/	+/pʰrata/	tearing

/b/

+/bɟ/	+/bɟara/	becoming thin; losing weight
+/bz/	+/bzaya/	boring; making a hole
+/bl/	+/blaya/	swallowing
+/br/	+/brasɪppa/	thimble

/t/

+/tp/	+/tpasa/	feeling oppressed e.g., because of heat	
+/tb/°	+/tbaya/	sinking	This is in free variation with +/db/
+/tq/°	+/tqara/	touching	This is in free variation with +/dq/
+/tx/	+/txana/	grinding	
+/ty/	+/tyapʰa/	bending	
+/tw/	+/twaxa/	crushing	
+/tl/	+/tlaya/	falling asleep	
+/tr/	+/traya/	driving	
+/tm/	+/tmaša/	submerging	

/tʰ/

+/tʰl/	+/tʰlama/	punishing
+/tʰm/	+/tʰmani/	eighty

/d/

+/dy/	+/dyara/	returning
+/dr/	+/draša/	arguing

NB. No clusters with /c/ as the first element.

/cʰ/

+/cʰtʰ/	+/cʰtʰara/	knotting

Lists of Stems Containing the Attested Emphatic Clusters

+/cʰx/	+/cʰxala/	dying the eyelids or eyelashes
+/cʰr/	+/cʰraza/	preaching
+/cʰm/	+/cʰmala/	becoming complete

/ɟ/

+/ɟz/	+/ɟzara/	filling up to the brim
+/ɟw/	+/ɟwara/	becoming large
+/ɟr/	+/ɟraya/	shaving

/q/

+/qt/	+/qtaya/	cutting off
+/qč/	+/qčaya/	cutting off
+/qy/	+/qyara/	coming off; peeling
+/qw/	+/qwara/	burying
+/qr/	+/qraya/	reading
+/qm/	+/qmata/	twining or twisting (e.g., a baby) in his bed; tying firmly

N.B. No cluster with /ʔ/ as the first element.

/č/

+/čy/	+/čyama/	shutting
+/čl/	+/člapʰa/	splitting; causing a rift
+/čr/	+/črapʰa/	knocking suddenly
+/čm/	+/čmača/	wilting

/čʰ/

+/čʰy/	+/čʰyara/	being on bad terms with

/ǰ/

+/ǰy/	+/ǰyara/	urinating
+/ǰr/	+/ǰraya/	flowing
+/ǰm/	+/ǰmaya/	coming together; convening

/s/

+/sp/	+/spay/	good
+/st/	+/stama/	falling down e.g., (roof)

+/sq/	+/sqata/	squatting; dying (in a "degrading sense")	
+/sx/	+/sxaya/	swimming	
+/sy/	+/syama/	fasting	
+/sw/	+/swaya/	feeling satisfied (hunger); dyeing	
+/sl/	+/slaya/	descending	
+/sr/	+/sraʰa/	burning e. g., (of pepper)	

/z/

+/zd/	+/zdaya/	feeling frightened	
+/zq/°	+/zqara/	knitting	This is in free variation with +/sq/
+/zy/	+/zyarat/	pilgrimage	
+/zl/	+/zlama/	treating unjustly	
+/zr/	+/zraya/	planting; sowing	
+/zm/	+/zmata/	filling up to the brim	

/š/

+/št/	+/štaxa/	lying on a flat surface
+/šx/	+/šxara/	becoming black
+/šy/	+/šyala/	coughing
+/šr/	+/šraya/	lamp
+/šm/	+/šmaya/	hearing

N.B. No clusters with /ž/ as the first element.

/x/

+/xt/	+/xtara/	beating harshly
+/xq/	+/xqara/	praising
+/xs/	+/xsara/	losing
+/xy/	+/xyata/	sewing
+/xw/	+/xwara/	white
+/xl/	+/xlawa/	milking
+/xr/	+/xraša/	deceiving
+/xm/	+/xmata/	needle
+/xn/	+/xnami/	relationship through marriage

/ġ/

+/ġd/	+/ġdara/	having a walk
+/ġz/	+/ġzada/	harvesting
+/ġl/	+/ġlaba/	winning

/h/

+/hcʰ/	+/hcʰama/	ruling

N.B. No clusters with /y/ as the first element.
No clusters with /ʮ/ as the first element.

/l/

+/lt/	+/ltaya/	licking up
+/lq/	+/lqata/	pecking; embroidering
+/ly/	+/lyasa/	chewing
+/lm/	+/lmasa/	sucking; absorbing

/r/

+/rpʰ/	+/rpʰaya/	becoming loose
+/rtʰ/	+/rtʰama/	pronouncing
+/rd/	+/rdaxa/	boiling
+/rq/	+/rqiʔa/	sky; firmament
+/rč/	+/rčaya/	smearing
+/rǰ/	+/rǰama/	throwing stones at
+/rš/	+/ršama/	marking
+/rx/	+/rxata/	running
+/ry/	+/ryada/	darning; stitching
+/rw/	+/rwaya/	becoming drunk

/m/

+/mt/	+/mtaya/	arriving
+/md/°	+/mdabrana/	person in charge
+/ms/	+/msaya/	being able
+/my/	+/myasa/	sucking
+/mr/	+/mraya/	becoming ill

		/n/
+/nt/	+/ntara/	protecting
+/ntʰ/	+/ntʰara/	falling down e.g., fruit or falling out hair
+/nd/	+/ndara/	vowing; devoting
+/nq/	+/nqara/	engraving
+/ns/	+/nsawa/	planting
+/nz/	+/nzara/	making someone a nazarite
+/nš/	+/nšata/	skinning
+/nx/	+/nxala/	sifting
+/ny/	+/nyasa/	biting
+/nw/	+/nwaya/	gushing out; welling forth

CHAPTER VI

STRESS AND INTONATION

6.1. *Introductory Remarks*

Stress and intonation are two of the most important components of language. Their significance is not only confined to the shaping of the rhythm and the melody; in many languages they demonstrate some intricate grammatical and semantic functions. Both are suprasegmental (prosodic) features whose relevance is usually associated with a syllable, as the shortest unit in speech, and the sentence, as the longest unit.

In linguistic studies, these prosodic elements have received far less attention than the segmental elements simply because the latter are more tangible by virtue of their easily identifiable nature. They have become even more tangible and identifiable in languages that are reduced to writing. In writing, especially an alphabetic one, the major target has been to assign symbols to segments only. Few languages have cared to incorporate the prosodic features of language in their writing systems. It is only in the recent years that stress and intonation began to draw the attention of linguists. Nowadays, no study of a given language could be complete and coherent if its prosodic aspects are left untouched. NA language is not an exception in this regard. Some investigators have touched on the issue of word-stress but sentence-stress, rhythm and intonation have remained, more or less, totally neglected. It is, therefore, necessary to gear our attention to these virgin aspects of NA. This chapter is only an initial attempt in this direction. Some interesting aspects will be brought to light for the first time, but much is left for future investigation.

6.2. *Stress and Rhythm*

Stress could have different interpretations from the speaker's or the listener's standpoints. When the speaker's activity in producing stressed syllables is in focus, stress may be defined in terms of greater effort that enters into the production of a stressed syllable as opposed to an unstressed syllable (Lehiste, 1970:106). But when the stress is defined from the listener's standpoint, the claim is often made that stressed syllables are louder than the unstressed syllables (ibid). This is why Ladefoged (1982) tends to think that stress can always be defined in terms of something a speaker does while it is difficult to define it from the listener's point of view (p. 104). To avoid those complications, it would suffice to deal with stress in terms of greater or lesser physiological effort on the part of the speaker and greater or lesser prominence on the part of the listener who assesses prominence as the overall index of greater loudness and length and higher pitch.

Stress is, hence, primarily the result of greater physiological effort exerted by the speaker at a certain point within a polysyllabic word and at repeated points within the flow of speech. A greater respiratory effort makes a given syllable more prominent and with the decrease in this effort syllables diminish in prominence. A realistic division of the prominence continuum is to identify three degrees of prominence to be associated with the trichotomy of weakly stressed, medium stressed and strongly stressed syllables. However, the dichotomy of unstressed and stressed syllables has customarily been more dominant. No doubt, the term "unstressed" is only figuratively employed to subsume the first two degrees of stress because literally the term is meaningless since no portion of speech is produced without physiological effort; consequently, every portion should have some prominence. In other words, the unstressed syllables stand for the portions with minimum prominence.

It is possible to distinguish between stress assignment within a word and within a sentence because within the latter it is likely for words to undergo a shift in the location of stress or to emerge with partial stress only. Within a word–excluding the monosyllabic ones–a certain syllable sounds more striking in relation to others, while in a sentence certain words sound more striking in relation to the rest. The former case is called *word stress* and the latter *sentence stress*.

Languages differ in the manner they use word stress and sentence stress to signal linguistic and non-linguistic variations. Some languages show a strong trend of retaining the stress on a certain syllable within the word regardless of the syllabic structure and the number of syllables. Obviously, in such cases stress becomes highly predictable. Czech words nearly always have the stress on the first syllable irrespective of the number of the syllables (Ladefoged, 1982:224). In other languages, stress changes its place according to several factors, foremost of all are the number of the syllables, their internal structure and arrangement within a word, the grammatical category of words and their status as native or loan words. Even within this category of languages, stress could be predictable if the restructuring of words through affixation shows a strong tendency to retain the stress on the same syllable away from either end of the word boundary. To facilitate the rules of stress assignment, linguists use the classificatory terms of ultimate, penultimate, and antepenultimate to identify the structural location of stress. If no rules could be formulated or if the rules can capture only certain instances leaving the rest of the instances unaccounted for without some ad hoc rules, then the predictability of stress becomes less likely and its role as a distinctive feature between the lexical items increases.

If stress is highly predictable its function is primarily that of determining the rhythm and the overall pronunciation though it still can have a demarcative function i.e., it helps to signal the word boundary (Hyman, 1975:205). In languages in which stress resists straightforward predictability, the functions of stress are no longer confined to pronunciation and demarcation; it can assume a wide and diversified range of lexical and grammatical functions.

The distribution of stressed and unstressed syllable within a language determines its *rhythm*. A language can either be *stress-timed* or *syllable-timed.* In a stress-timed language a maximum expiratory force is exerted on certain syllables which form the beats; the beats tend to recur at regular intervals (Pike, 1966; Abercrombie, 1967; Ladefoged, 1982). In other words those beats or stressed syllables tend to be temporally equidistant. The space between each two beats is filled with anything from no to several unstressed syllables. English and Arabic are essentially stress-timed languages. In a syllable-timed language the expiratory force is evenly distributed on all syllables thus all syllables form beats. Japanese is a typically syllable-timed language; French, Spanish and Italian also fall into the same category.

All the above stress and rhythmic attributes assigned to languages do not have absolute values. The dichotomies of free/fixed, predictable/unpredictable stress and that of stress-timed and syllable-timed rhythms may overlap to different extents. Consequently, it would be more realistic to consider the members of each dichotomy as the extreme ends on a continuum between which other languages exist with greater or lesser tendency towards one of the polar points.

6.3. *Stress and Rhythm in the Koine*

Concerning the free/fixed continuum of stress, the Koine falls somewhere between its two polar ends in that stress can occur in all three structural positions in a word i.e., initial, medial and final. Nevertheless, the freedom of stress assignment is greatly restricted by a strong tendency to keep the stress in the penultimate position within a word and even more so within a *stem*. This restriction reduces the likelihood of stress being phonemic in the Koine. Due to this fact, it is quite difficult to find lexical items that are solely and radically distinguished on the basis of stress. The few instances that are contrastive in stress represent grammatical constructs rather than lexical items. They could be verbal pieces with/without objects, cases with/without the possessive 3rd person plural suffix and polysyllabic question words indicating different attitudes.

(a)

VERBAL PIECES WITHOUT OBJECTS		VERBAL PIECES WITH OBJECTS	
/ˈmɪxyena/	They have beaten	/mɪxˈyena/	They have beaten them.
/ˈmɪxyeɥɪn/	I have beaten	/mɪxˈyeɥɪn/	I have beaten them.
/pʰaˈruqelɪ/	He is finishing	/pʰaruˈqelɪ/	He is finishing them.
/pʰaˈruqeɥɪn/	I am finishing	/pʰaruˈqeɥɪn/	I am finishing them.

(b)

WITHOUT POSSESSIVE PRONOUNS		WITH POSSESSIVE PRONOUNS	
/ˈnašelɪ/	He is a man	/naˈšelɪ/	He is their man (relative)
/ˈɟurelɪ/	He is big	/ɟuˈrelɪ/	He is their big (boss or chief)
/ˈcʰalbelɪ/	It is a dog	/cʰalˈbelɪ/	It is their dog
/ˈsurelɪ/	He is small (young)	/suˈrelɪ/	He is their smallest (youngest)

(c)

STRAIGHTFORWARD QUESTIONS		EXCLAMATORY QUESTIONS[1]	
/ˈmudi/ = [ˈmu:di]	What...?	/muˈdi/ = [muˈdi:]	What... (implying surprise and demanding clarification)?!
/qaˈmudi/ = [qaˈmu:di]	Why...?	/qamuˈdi/ = [qamuˈdi:]	Why...?!

---

[1] For further details on the so-called Exclamatory Questions see 6.5. below.

6.4. *Word Stress and Stem Stress*

Dealing with stress in the Koine in terms of "words" will complicate the issue partly because of the ensuing increase in the irregularity of stress placement and partly because of the difficulty in identifying and defining the "word" per se. In the Koine, as well as in many other languages, a word can stand for a monosyllabic morpheme and for a complete sentence. The preposition /mɪn/ is a word and /mɪxˈyelan/, which looks like a word, is, in fact, a sentence meaning "We have beaten them."

A more practical approach to stress would be its treatment in terms of the "stem" itself or in relation to the suffixes. The notion of stem stress is identical with Krotokoff's *Primary Stress* applied in the analysis of the NA dialect of *Aradhin* (Krotkoff, 1982). Assessing the stress within the stem and in relation to the first suffix is of prime importance because stress shuns the suffixes and hardly ever goes beyond the boundary of stem. In this manner the penultimate rule will become extremely powerful because it will capture the overwhelming majority of cases. Instances like /pʰuˈrɪqloxun/ "you have finished" and /pʰuˈrɪqqaloxun/ "you had finished" will not be having the stress on the antepenultimate and preantepenultimate syllables but rather on the penultimate one in relation to the first suffixed syllable. By the same token, stress in /ˈʔɪtʰqaloxun/ "you had" is not irregular. In all the derivations of /ʔɪt/ "there is," stress must be penultimate in relation to the first suffix because the root is monosyllabic. And if in /pʰaˈruqetʰun/ "you are finishing" and /pʰaˈruqetʰunqa/ "you were finishing" the stress is not penultimate in relation to the first suffixed syllable, it is because these verbal pieces, and several others, contrast with /pʰaruˈqetʰun/ "you are finishing them" and /pʰaruˈqetʰunqa/ "you were finishing them", a case mentioned earlier on in 6.3.a.

According to this analysis, many of the so-called antepenultimate and preantepenultimate stresses in verbal pieces (Maclean, 1895; Tsereteli, 1978) will turn out to be penultimate ones. Nevertheless, no matter how uniform the penultimate rule is, there will still remain some isolated cases that resist this pattern. These could be loan or native words, former compounds and other expressions. Notice the examples

(a) Loanwords that have resisted naturalization:

LOANWORD		LOANWORD	
/ʔalbaˈʔal/	immediately	/ˈsarsari/	person with bad manners
/ˈmasalan/	for example	+/ˈxulasa/	finally; in brief
/ˈnaɟɪstan/	suddenly	/ˈǰamiʕa/	university
/ˈhammaša/	always	+/ˈhaspital/	hospital

(b) Adverbs ending with the suffix /ʔit/ have ultimate stress:

ADVERB
/pʰriša'ʔit/   especially
/cʰullana'ʔit/   generally
/šitʰa'ʔit/   annually
/yarxa'ʔit/   monthly
/yuma'ʔit/   daily

(c) Adverbs and adverbial expressions have antepenultimate stress:

ADVERB
/'bazzunɪ/   last year
+/'barayɪ/   outside
/'ɟaqayɪ/   inside
+/'xaraya/   last
+/'mudalɪ/   together
/'pʰipʰalɟa/   in the middle
/'qamaya/   first

(d) Words with the possessive 3rd P. Pl. suffix receive an ultimate stress. This stressing is the result of the deletion of a syllable which was originally there and is still retained in writing.

WORDS	POSSESSIVE CASE	
/ʔa'xuna/	/ʔaxu'ne/	their brother
/ʔaxun'qatʰɪ/	/ʔaxunqa'tʰe/	their brothers

(e) The days of the week Monday through Thursday have an antepenultimate stress:

DAYS
/'tʰrošiba/   Monday
+/'tlošiba/   Tuesday
+/ʔar'pošiba/   Wednesday
/xam'šošiba/   Thursday

(f) The geographical directions have an antepenultimate stress. This is the result of breaking up an unfamiliar sequence of consonants by an epenthetic vowel that increases the number of syllables by one thus rendering the stress antepenultimate.

DIRECTIONS
/'madɪnxa/   East

+/ˈmaʔɪrwa/ West
+/ˈɹarbɪya/ North
/ˈtʰaymɪna/ South

In spite of the above irregular stressing, the penultimate rule holds predominantly. Many of the irregularities among the native words are the result of compounding as shown in the next section.

6.5. *Stress in Longer Pieces*

In longer stretches of speech, stress may be reduced (from primary to secondary), shifted (from one syllable to another even without affixation) and deleted completely. Those phenomena act jointly to determine the nature of rhythm in the Koine, a topic to be discussed in the next section. However, in preparation for that let us demonstrate some of the dynamics of stress in compound words and other short utterances.

In compounds, one of the primary stresses is reduced to secondary if the two components are content words and are non-monosyllabic; if, however, one of them is a function word or simply a monosyllabic, the compound emerges with only a primary stress without the secondary stress. Notice the examples:

/ˈxamša # ˈšabba/	→ /xamˈšoˌšiba/	= Thursday (applicable to Monday through Thursday)
+/ˈxwara # ˈdɪqna/[2]	→ +/ˌxwarˈdɪqna/	= elderly
+/ˈqɪšta # ˈmaran/	→ +/ˌqɪštiˈmaran/	= rainbow
/ˈɹarma # ˈpʰila/	→ /ˌɹramˈpʰila/	= ivory
+/ˈʔazla # ˈcʰušɪ/	→ +/ˌʔazlaˈcʰušɪ/	= spider
/ˈpʰarxa # ˈlelɪ/	→ /ˌpʰarxaˈlelɪ/	= butterfly
/ˈšal # ˈqdala/	→ /ˌšalɪˈqdala/	= scarf
/ˈbɪ(t) # ˈpʰalɹa/	→ /ˈpʰipʰalɹa/	= in between; in the middle
/b # ˈʔan # ˈzaqnɪ/	→ /ˈbazzunɪ/	= last year
/ˈla # ˈxšixa/	→ /ˈlaxšixa/	= useless; mean

It is not unreasonable to assume that many of the irregular stresses in long words could be associated with compounding that stipulates stress reduction and stress shift.

---

2 Emphasis is restricted mainly to +/xwara/, +/maran/ and +/ʔazla/.

The polysyllabic cardinal numerals receive different stressing when used strictly as numerals as opposed to modifiers in a nominal phrase.

NUMERAL		NOMINAL PHRASE	
+/ˈʔarpa/	four	+/ʔarˈpa ˈnašɪ/	four men
/ˈxamša/	five	/xamˈša ˈnašɪ/	five men
/ˈʔɪšta/	six	/ʔɪšˈta qaˈlamɪ/	six pencils

Instances sensitive to stress dynamics are not restricted to the above compounds and the numerals. Other more complicated cases are readily available. Compare the examples below:

/ˈraba # ˈjura # ˈʔilɪ/	→ /ˈraba ˈjurelɪ/	= It is very big.
	→ /ˌraba ˈjurelɪ/	= How big it is!
/ˈxa # ˈyala/	→ /ˈxa ˈyala/	= one boy
	→ /ˌxa ˈyala/	= a boy
/ˈxa # ˈxina/	→ /ˈxaxina/	= one more
	→ /xaˈxina/	= someone (thing) else
/ˈxa # ˈjahɪ # ˈxitʰa/	→ /ˈxajaˌxitʰa/	= once more
	→ /ˌxajaˈxitʰa/	= some other time
/ˈcʰma # šaxina # ˈʔilɪ/	→ /ˈcʰma šaˈxinelɪ/	= How hot is it?
	→ /ˌcʰma šaˈxinelɪ/	= How hot it is!

The most interesting case involves the polysyllabic question words. The difference between these words in straightforward interrogatives and interrogatives implying great surprise or suspicion and demanding a repetition or clarification, is that in the former they receive a primary stress and in the latter a secondary stress. For convenience, they will, henceforth, be distinguished as questions and exclamatory questions and punctuated by a question mark "?" and a question mark followed by an exclamation mark "?!," respectively.

QUESTIONS		EXCLAMATORY QUESTIONS	
/ˈmudi ˌmɪrrux/	What did you say?	/ˌmudi ˈmɪrrux/	What did you say?!
/ˈʔicʰa ˌxɪšlux/	Where did you go?	/ˌicʰa ˈxɪšlux/	Where did you go?!

Obviously the questions have a falling intonation as opposed to the falling-rising intonation for the exclamatory questions. However, when question words are used in their citation (isolation) form, stress in exclamatory questions becomes ultimate instead of penultimate. This is a perfect example of the interaction between stress and pitch.

QUESTIONS		EXCLAMATORY QUESTIONS	
/ˈmudi/	What...?	/muˈdi/	What...?!

/qaˈmudi/	Why...?	/qamuˈdi/	Why...?!
/ˈʔichₐ/	Where...?	/ʔiˈchₐ/	Where...?!

As indicated earlier on, all those changes in stressing and the deletion of stress, which take place more frequently in longer sentences, will be important factors in determining the nature of rhythm in the Koine.

6.6. Rhythm in the Koine

As for the nature of rhythm in the Koine, there are strong indications suggesting a stress-timed rhythm as in Arabic and English. The space between two adjacent beats is filled with unstressed syllables which could even include content words potentially eligible for stress. A careful examination of the following utterances, where the bars delimit the beats,

(1) /ˈxa | ˈyala | bılˈqašeqa | ˈjullu/ = One boy (only) was putting on his clothes.
(2) /xa ˈyala | bılˈqašeqa | ˈjullu/ = A boy was putting on his clothes.
(3) /ˈʔithlan | bathˈqathı | ʔaˈthiqı | qxathı/ = We have old and new houses.
(4) /bzoˈniqaloxun | ʔathnaˈbelı/ = They would have bought you cars.
(5) /bzoˈniqaloxun | xamša ʔıšˈta | bathˈqathı/ = They would have bought you five or six houses.

shows that 0–6 unstressed syllables intervene between two beats. Those intervening syllables are associated with the preceding and following beats in the form of rhythmic groups. Although the association is frequently congruent with the divisions indicating the grammatical constituents, violations of that congruency is not unlikely. In utterance 5, /xamša ʔıšta/ is grammatically subordinate of /bathqathı/ yet the rhythmic constraints impose their ascription to two separate rhythmic groups.

Each rhythmic group tends to last for an equal period of time thus rendering the occurrence of the beats isochronous. But how is the isochronism brought about if the beats are separated by a different number of syllables? Tempo adjustments seem to be the major device in accomplishing the isochronism. The speaker usually lingers on the stressed syllables (beats) and speeds up on the unstressed ones. Both slowing down and speeding up cannot be effective without some phonetic changes, most important of which are vowel lengthening or shortening and tense or nontense (lax) execution of consonants. In tense sounds the period during which the articulatory organs maintain the appropriate configuration is relatively long, while in nontense sounds, the entire gesture is executed in a somewhat superficial manner (Chomsky & Halle, 1968:324). Thus stressed syllables are more tensely articulated and stretched in time while the unstressed ones are slurred over and compressed in time. The vocalic maneuvering is far more influential in this respect. This probably accounts for the phonetic presence of three vowel lengths in the Koine. In an open stressed syllable, vowels usually demonstrate maximum length: if such a syllable loses its stress, the vowel could be relatively or extremely shortened depending on its position in the utterance. The second vowel /a/ in +/ʔatʰˈnabɪl/ "car" is very long because it occurs in an open stressed syllable. When the word is rendered plural +/ʔatʰnaˈbelɪ/, stress advances by one syllable and /a/ still manages to retain some length (medium) due to the openness of the syllable and its adjacency to the main stress. However, the same vowel becomes extremely short when further suffixes are added viz., +/ʔatʰnabeˈloxun/.

6.7. Pitch Patterns: Tones and Intonations

In speech there is always a continuous change in the fundamental frequency which is auditorily realized as *pitch*. Languages use pitch in two essentially different ways. If it signals semantic differences between words, the languages are called *tone languages*. Many of the African and Asian languages fall into this category. Languages in which pitch has no specific role in the semantic shaping of words but is rather used to signal a combination of syntactic, semantic and attitudinal features of the utterance, are *intonation languages*.

Tone and intonation languages are not always mutually exclusive. Swedish is basically an intonation language, but it also makes use of a restricted tone system (Fry, 1968:367). Moreover, tone languages may also make use of pitch in a way similar to intonation languages (O'Connor, 1973:262). In tone languages the function of intonation is, as it were, superimposed upon and may modify the working of the phonological tone system (Fry, 1968:367). Despite all this overlapping, a general distinction between the two categories of languages is readily made. The following quotation from Abercrombie (1967:105) provides a succinct distinction:

Tone is speech melody when it is a property of the word, while intonation is speech melody when it is the property of a sentence. This means that in a tone language a change of speech melody is likely to change the meaning of individual words, whereas in an intonation language a change of speech melody is likely to change the meaning of the sentence as a whole.

6.8. *Pitch Patterns in the Koine*

There is little to be said about the particularity of the linguistic/nonlinguistic manipulation of pitch in this dialect. The Koine is unequivocally an intonation language since pitch is never used to signal differences between lexical items. Like most of the intonation languages, the Koine makes a frequent use of five primary pitch variations: low-fall, high-fall, low-rise, high-rise and fall-rise. The rise-fall is less frequently attested as is the case in most of the intonation languages. They all serve a combination of syntactic, semantic and attitudinal functions at the sentential level.

6.8.1. Falling Pitch Patterns

The falling pitch patterns, both low and high, have the general purpose of expressing an utterance with a sense of completeness so that the attention of the listener is no longer required inasmuch as that particular utterance is concerned. The high-fall usually indicates a more vigorous and determinate notion of completeness and finality than the low-fall does.

The low-fall is commonly associated with the following types of utterances:

(a) Statements

/xa yala cʰɪryelɪ/ = He is a short boy.

(b) Unemphatic imperatives

/pʰtʰuxlɪ sanduqa/ = Open the box!

(c) Interrogatives with question-words

/mudi bzamrɪtʰ/ = What will you sing?

The high-fall is commonly associated with the following types of utterances:

(a) Emphatic imperatives

/ruq tʰilun pʰolisɪ/ = Run! The police came.

(b) Declarative utterances implying an important message that stipulates actions to be taken

/+[matran] dulɪ bɪtʰaya/ = The Archbishop is coming (i.e., be ready)

(c) Exclamations

/cʰma ɟurelɪ/ = How big it is!

6.8.2. *Rising Pitch Patterns*

These pitch patterns, unlike the falling patterns, imply a sense of the incompleteness of the utterance as if further information is expected from the speaker or a response is necessary on the part of the listener.

The low-rise is associated with:

(a) Subordinate clauses in conditional sentences (principal clauses have a low-fall pitch)

/ʔɪn šat^{h}ɪtt^{h}ɪ +[dɪrmanux].../ = If you take (drink) your medicine,...

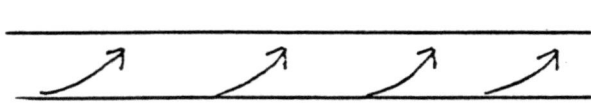

(b) Comments that a listener makes when preparing to take turn in a conversation

/he/... Yes, /he/... Yes, +/spay/... O.K. /mudi/ What...

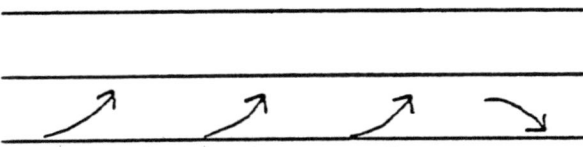

(c) Enumeration or pronouncing items in a series (viz., alphabet characters; shopping list) when the enumeration and pronunciation are performed slowly so as to be followed by other activities (writing, memorization). All the items will have a low-rise except the last which will terminate the activity with a low-fall.

/xabuši/ "apples", /banani/ "bananas," /ɟillali/ "vegetables," /laxma/ "and bread"

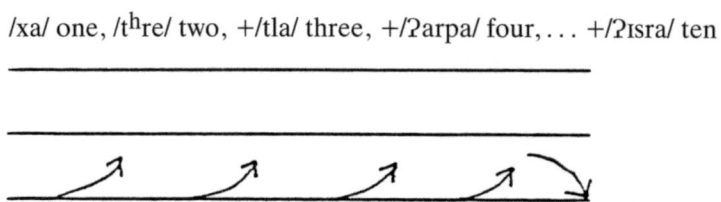

The high-rise has a very important and straightforward role in the Koine not only because it marks the questions that demand a "Yes/No" answer but also because this pattern of pitch is the only device to formulate this kind of questions. In other words no syntactic readjustments are required as is the case in formal English. Compare the examples below:

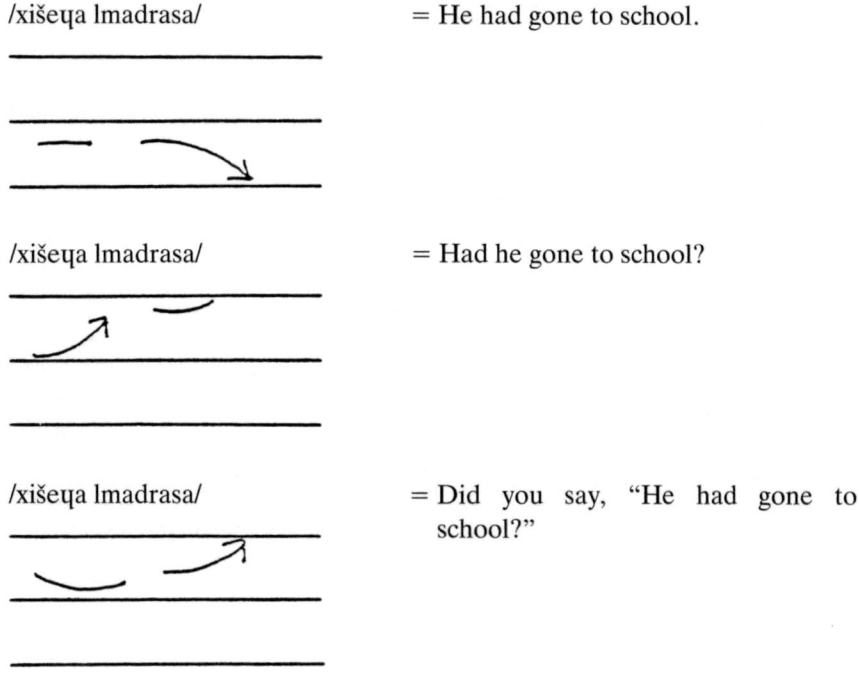

The above three examples show that the difference between the first utterance and the last two lies in the direction of pitch while the difference between the last two is in the timing of the pitch change. The change in direction is made in combination with the primary stress which both together indicate the point of greatest significance in speech.

6.8.3. Fall-Rise Pitch Pattern

This pitch pattern is used to formulate the exclamatory questions mentioned in 6.5. The falling portion of the pitch is usually from medium height to low while the rising one is from low to high; however, the rise is not acute, i. e., it rises gradually. Notice the examples:

mudi = What?!

cʰma yumanɪ = How many days?!

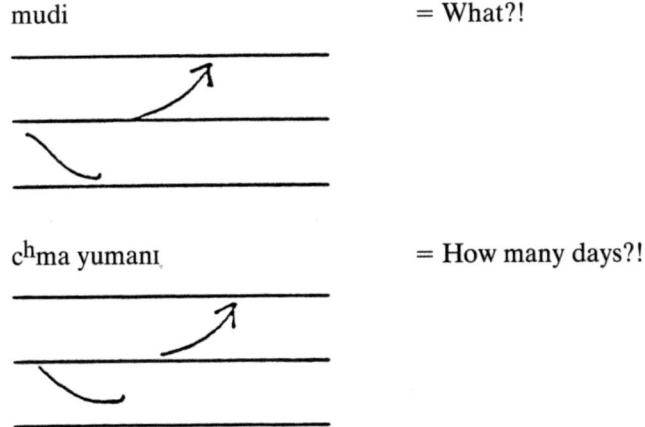

CHAPTER VII

METHODS AND INSTRUMENTATION

7.1. Material and General Experimental Procedures

All the sounds of the Koine have been subjected, in one way or another, to experimental investigation. The general procedure for the collection of data was to select suitable words with segments of interest and place them in an appropriate carrier sentence which in this case was: /c^{h}t^{h}u ... t^{h}reɟa/ meaning "write ... twice." The main idea behind using a carrier sentence, instead of pronouncing words in their citation form, is that in the latter case one may lose the real sentential or phrasal context which facilitates closer control of every feature, provides greater consistency and renders the sounds more natural, particularly, inasmuch as stress and intonation are concerned.

With every set of sounds, the token words containing them were randomized and then pronounced repeatedly in the carrier sentence. The aim was to produce five tokens of each sound, but because of occasional technical failure the wanted number was not always attained.

7.2. Major Experiments

The experimental work comprised Spectrography, Airflow and Intraoral Pressure Measurements, Glottography, Laryngography and some limited use of the Thyrometer. In the next few pages the reader will find some information about each procedure and the way it works in analyzing speech.

7.2.1. Spectrography

The general aim is to observe speech displayed in the form of acoustic energy. Such a display allows the identification of the nature of speech both in terms of source features (i.e., voice, noise, transient and a gap in case of the absence of a source) and resonator features (i.e., occlusive, fricative, nasal, vowel-like etc.). Horizontally, a spectrogram displays time while vertically frequency is displayed. Both together help in measuring the duration of a particular segment or subsegment and the level of the frequency at a particular point in time. These measurements being available, one can obtain valuable information about the manner and place of articulation of all segments, measure their duration fairly adequately and detect other significant features. The intensity of the sound is detected from the darkness or the lightness of the acoustic signal.

7.2.2. Airflow Measurements

By knowing the volume of airflow through the mouth and the presence or absence of airflow through the nose, one is capable of obtaining information about the constrictions along the vocal tract, their locations, their approximate sizes and their timing. The information about those aspects will enable the investigator to form a good picture about the aerodynamic conditions which in turn can contribute in explaining many aspects of speech production.

Airflow traces were made available by using the Electro-Aerometer which consists of a mask fitted to the mouth and nose. The air passes through four one-way rubber valves that are easily opened. They measure separately airflow into and out of the mouth and into and out of the nose. The opening of the valves depends on the volume of the passing air. On the opposite sides of the rubber valves there is a light and a photoelectric cell. The amount of light depends on the volume flow rate of air through the rubber valve. Thus the light is converted into electric signals which set the writing instrument into action.

7.2.3. Intraoral Pressure Measurements

The intraoral pressure experiments were conducted to obtain information about the pressure build-up patterns as well as the extent of their peaks. The information is helpful in shedding light on supraglottal and glottal apertures together with the supraglottal and glottal activities during articulation.

Pressure was measured by inserting a polyethylene tube, with an external diameter of about 3 mm, through the nose into the pharynx to avoid interferences with normal articulation which are likely when the tube is placed in the mouth. The distance between the position of the free end of the tube and the nares was about 12–14 cm. The compressed air behind the stricture was transferred through the polyethylene tube to a pressure transducer by two small holes near the free end of the tube.

The combination of airflow measurements and intraoral pressure readings are most helpful in explaining the underlying aerodynamic conditions of speech production.

7.2.4. Glottography

A Photo-Electric Glottograph was used to monitor the glottal aperture and the horizontal glottal activity. To obtain glottograms, a flexible tube, containing a phototransducer, had to be inserted through the nose into the pharynx. Strong light was focused on the larynx from the outside so as to shine through its tissues beneath the vocal folds. The light is picked up by the phototransducer only when the vocal folds are open; the wider opening of the folds means that more light falls on the phototransducer so that there is a bigger electrical signal. A small electrical signal stands for limited abduction and the absence of the signal indicates an adduction. We usually obtain the following types of glottograms, Fig. 9.

In Fig. 9, left to right, the large pulse above the baseline with no ripples means that the glottis is wide open with no vibration; this glottogram is representative of voiceless (aspirated) sounds. The small pulse with no ripples means that the glottis is only relatively open especially at the initial phase of the sound and voicing is inhibited due to a tense glottis; this is common with voiceless unaspirated sounds. When there are ripples only, that means the glottis is adducted and the vocal folds are vibrating; this is typical of voiced sounds. The absence of any pulse above the baseline means that the glottis is adducted as in a glottal stop.

7.2.5. Laryngograph

The laryngograph consists of two superficially applied electrodes that are placed on either side of the larynx. An oscillator provides a signal source of one Mega Hz which is fed to an electrode on one side of the larynx, the other electrode picks up the signal and transfers it to a detector. The detector and the ancillary circuitry measure the attenuation of the signal between the electrodes. In function this device is similar to the glottograph though the approach is different.

7.2.6. Thyrometer

It was used to indicate the presence or absence of laryngeal elevation or depression. The thyrometer consists of a light source that casts a narrow beam of light onto a small mirror stuck to the skin of the neck over the notch of the thyroid. A photocell detects the light beam reflected by the mirror. The tilting of the mirror resulting from the movement of the larynx causes changes in the angle of the reflection of the light beam. The transmitted light beam is detected by the photocell. In a certain way the vertical movement of the thyroid cartilage is detected electrically and calibrated. Even if calibration is not done, as in our case, the overall estimation of the elevation or depression is fairly easily determined.

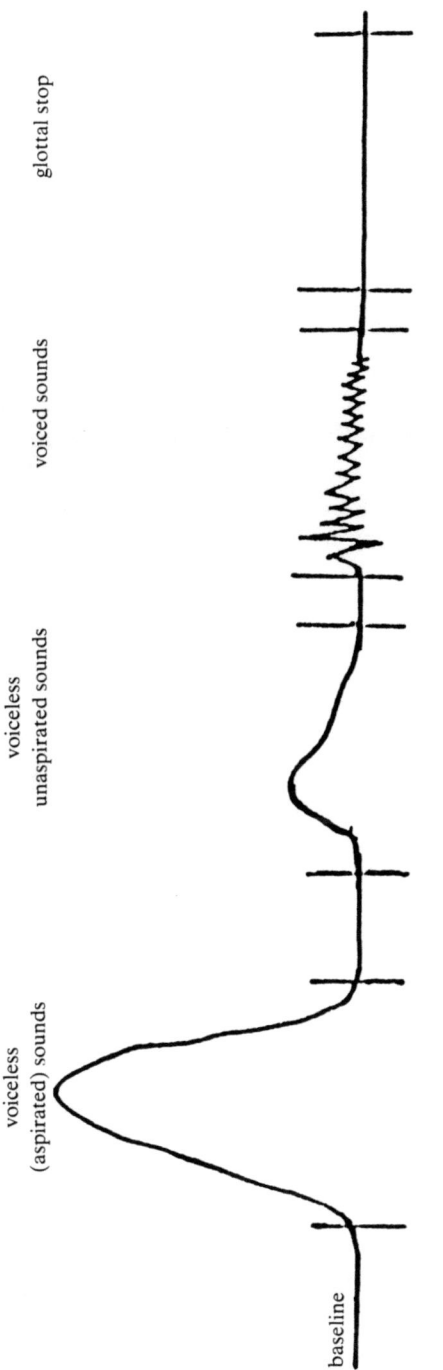

Fig. 9. A schematic representation of the types of glottograms

CHAPTER VIII

ARTICULATORY, AERODYNAMIC AND ACOUSTIC DESCRIPTION OF CONSONANTS

8.1. Introductory Remarks

This chapter is a statement about the articulatory, aerodynamic and acoustic features of each consonant. The articulatory description involves the glottal aperture and activity, the location of the supraglottal strictures and the vertical movement of the larynx when data are available. The aerodynamic description covers the intraoral pressure pulse and the peak values to be explained in coordination with the articulatory observations. The acoustic identification is exclusively based on spectrographic investigation.[1]

8.2. Plosive Production

Before embarking on the description of each consonant, it is instructive for the reader to acquaint himself with the most recurrent terminology that is part of the description of the underlying structure of plosive sounds production. The description is in line with Fant (1958; 1960; 1973) and Klatt (1973) in recognizing four phases: stop–explosion–frication–aspiration. But to avoid certain inevitable difficulties of delineation, phases two and three are occasionally merged as Klatt has already done. Although it is difficult to delineate phases three and four, the cues suggested by Fant (1960) greatly minimize the difficulty.

According to Fant (1958:307–8)

a *stop period* represents the time when the active articulator is in a considerably tight contact with the passive articulator. The *explosion* represents the sudden release of the tight contact leading, in its turn, to the sudden release of an over-pressure which creates the explosion.

Such a sudden release of pressure produces a sort of noise that is called *transient* (Fant, 1960:18). The *frication segment* represents the escape of air through the gradually widening constriction resulting from the movement of the articulator

---

1 For samples of experimental evidence see the Appendix.

away from the target area. The noise here is turbulent and originates from random disturbances of the airflow resulting from the air being forced through a very narrow constriction (ibid.). The last phase, *aspiration,* or open aspiration as Fant prefers to call, is produced with greater articulatory opening than members of the class of fricative sounds (Fant, 1960:19).

Frication and aspiration, as defined by Fant

may occur simultaneously or in succession, or only one of the two noise categories may be chiefly present. But in the noise interval of a stop, assuming an increasing degree of opening, aspiration must follow frication if both are present. Aspiration is usually of lower intensity above 4000 Hz.

8.3. *Bilabial Plosives*

/b/ = Voiced Bilabial Plosive
/p/ = Voiceless Unaspirated Bilabial Plosive
/p^h/ = Voiceless Aspirated Bilabial Plosive

8.3.1. Voiced Bilabial Plosive, /b/

Articulatory and Aerodynamic Description. The glottis is adducted and the aerodynamic conditions are favorable for the vibration of the vocal folds. The uvula is raised to block the nasal passage. The adducted glottis creates high impedance in the way of airflow thus causing a gradual and low build-up of intraoral pressure. This aerodynamic condition helps the maintenance of vibration throughout most of the stop period though vibration becomes weaker towards the end of the stricture. Pressure is relieved with the release of the bilabial occlusion causing a reinforcement of the vibration in the following segment. Lip contact is not as forceful as in the voiceless unaspirated plosive /p/.

Acoustic Description. On a spectrogram the bilabial occlusion is represented by the absence of energy forming a segment of about 95 ms wide. The stop phase for /b/ is shorter than for both /p/ and /p^h/. A distinctive feature of /b/ is the presence of a voice bar at the baseline indicating the voiced nature of this sound. The spike representing the release of the stricture is less distinct than in /p/ and /p^h/ and this is basically attributed to low intraoral pressure. Voice striations are seen almost immediately after the release of the stricture. F_1 and F_2 values are roughly in the range of 250–300 Hz and 1250–1350 Hz, respectively.

8.3.2. Voiceless Unaspirated Bilabial Plosive, /p/

Articulatory and Aerodynamic Description. The glottis is adducted almost throughout the whole duration of the bilabial stricture. It is only slightly and temporarily open during the initial phase of the occlusion. Some elevation of the larynx is observed. The myodynamic and aerodynamic conditions in the form of great muscular tension and high intraoral pressure inhibit the vibration during the occlusion. Vibration commences immediately with or soon after the release of the occlusion. The soft palate is raised and the lips are pressed together perhaps more tightly than for /b/ and /p^h/. The lips and the cheeks are drawn somewhat inwards. The intraoral pressure is considerably high for a sound with minimum glottal abduction, a fact that might be attributed to the tense nature of /p/.

Acoustic Description. The tight bilabial stricture and the tense nature of /p/ is reflected on the spectrogram in the form of a wide blank column with a mean duration of 133 ms. The release, marked by the spike, is more distinct than for /b/. The spike is more noticeable at the level of the formants. Voicing resumes immediately or shortly after the release with a mean delay of 10 ms. The short delay in voice onset qualifies /p/ as an unaspirated sound. Formant values are within the range for /b/.

8.3.3. Voiceless Aspirated Bilabial Plosive, /p^h/

Articulatory and Aerodynamic Description. The glottis is abducted throughout the greater part of the bilabial stricture. The glottal stricture is too wide to cause any vibration. The open glottis at the instant of release and after it is the main reason behind the aspirative nature of this sound. The bilabial contact is less tense than for its unaspirated counterpart. Pressure is considerably high and is jointly attributed to the open glottis and the simultaneous nasal and oral occlusions.

Acoustic Description. The stop phase is indicated by a wide blank column with a mean duration of about 118 ms. The spike of the articulatory release is less distinct than for its unaspirated counterpart. The open glottis at the instant of release and for a while after it always delays the proper onset of voicing in the following vowel that accounts for the aspirative nature of /p^h/. The mean VOT value is 53 ms comprising the frication segment followed by aspiration. The VOT segment in /p^h/ is consistently shorter than in /t^h/ and /c^h/, a feature that is essentially attributed to the difference in the vector of contact between the active and passive articulators in those three aspirated sounds. F_1 and F_2 values are identical with those of /b/ and /p/.

8.4. Alveolar Plosives

/d/ = Voiced Alveolar Plosive
/t/ = Voiceless Unaspirated Alveolar Plosive
/t^h/ = Voiceless Aspirated Alveolar Plosive

8.4.1. Voiced Alveolar Plosive, /d/

Articulatory and Aerodynamic Description. The glottis is adducted and vibration is maintained throughout the whole duration of the alveolar stricture; as in /b/, vibration becomes slightly weaker towards the end of the stop phase due to the gradual build-up of pressure. The tongue is drawn forwards to execute the stricture against the alveolar ridge. The low pressure builds up gradually due to the impedence of an adducted glottis.

Acoustic Description. The persistence of voicing throughout the stop phase is indicated by the voice bar at the baseline. The absence of energy above the voice bar stands for the stop phase the mean duration of which is 103 ms. The release is indicated by a weak spike after which voice striations are reinforced in the following vowel. F_1 and F_2 values are 250 Hz and 1800–1900 Hz, respectively.

8.4.2. Voiceless Unaspirated Alveolar Plosive, /t/

Articulatory and Aerodynamic Description. The glottis is adducted throughout most part of the alveolar stricture. It is only slightly and temporarily open in the initial phase of the occlusion. Despite the constricted glottis, the myodynamic and aerodynamic conditions inhibit the vibration of the vocal folds. They resume vibration immediately or a short time after the release of the stricture. The tip of the tongue anchors firmly at the alveolar ridge and the complete occlusion causes a high build-up of pressure. The whole musculature of the tongue, pharynx and larynx is felt to be relatively tense; some laryngeal elevation is also observed. The tense articulation, laryngeal elevation and the initial abduction of the glottis all contribute in creating a high pressure.

Acoustic Description. The wide gap on the spectrogram stands for the stop phase with a mean duration of 120 ms. The release is more distinct than for its voiced counterpart and all the bilabial plosives. There is only a slight delay in the initiation of voicing after the release which justifies its description as unaspirated. Formant values are within the range for /d/.

8.4.3. Voiceless Aspirated Alveolar Plosive, /tʰ/

Articulatory and Aerodynamic Description. The glottis starts opening widely with the onset of the supraglottal stricture, therefore, it is wide open during the occlusion and for a while after it. The tip of the tongue is anchored in the same region of /t/, though less firmly. The complete occlusion and the wide spread glottis lead to a high build-up of pressure. Once the occlusion is relieved, the impounded air rushes across the open glottis and past the gradually increasing alveolar aperture. This causes turbulence noise at the supraglottal stricture and the glottis yielding frication and aspiration, consecutively. The vocal tract musculature is less tense than in /t/.

Acoustic Description. The stop phase lasts only 89 ms which is relatively shorter than for /t/. The difference seems to be the result of a tense articulation for /t/ and a less tense articulation for /tʰ/. The release is quite distinct especially at formant level. There is considerable delay in voicing after the release which renders the sound aspirated and at times even heavily aspirated. Formant values are within the same range of those for /d/ and /t/.

8.5. *Palatal Plosives*

/ɟ/ = Voiced Palatal Plosive
/c/ = Voiceless Unaspirated Palatal Plosive
/cʰ/ = Voiceless Aspirated Palatal Plosive

8.5.1. Voiced Palatal Plosive, /ɟ/

Articulatory and Aerodynamic Description. The glottis is adducted and vibration is maintained throughout the whole duration of the palatal stricture. The stricture is executed by raising the palatine dorsum towards the middle of the hard palate forming a complete occlusion that causes a low build-up of pressure due to the impedance of an adducted glottis. The area of contact for the palatal sounds is usually larger than the bilabial and alveolar sounds and the release is more sluggish.

Acoustic Description. The stop phase is only 79 ms. The voice bar at the baseline indicates the voiced nature of /ɟ/. Occasionally, the palatal plosives have more than one transient (spike). Despite the voiced nature of /ɟ/, voicing after the release is still delayed for a mean duration of 22 ms. This period is filled with a mixture of weak frication noise and weak voicing. The delay in the initiation of voicing is attributed to the sluggish release of the palatals in general. F_1 is very low and F_2 is very high. This yields a maximum separation of F_1 and F_2 and a maximum approximation of F_2 and F_3 which is typical with a stricture located in the palatal region. F_1, F_2 values are 250 Hz and 2000–2200 Hz, respectively.

8.5.2. Voiceless Unaspirated Palatal Plosive, /c/

Articulatory and Aerodynamic Description. The glottis ranges from being slightly abducted at the initial stage of the supraglottal stricture to an adducted glottis towards the end. The nature of the stricture is identical with that of /ɟ/ but less glottal impedance leads to a higher pressure for /c/. As in /ɟ/, the delay in the onset of vibration is, on average, greater than for plosives in a more anterior position i.e., bilabial and alveolar. Like the unaspirated /p/ and /t/, the whole musculature of the vocal tract is equally tense.

Acoustic Description. The relatively longer stop phase for /c/ than for its voiced counterpart is associated with the tense articulation of the former. Double spikes are characteristic of /c/ and the mean VOT is 28 ms. Formant values are identical with those of /ɟ/.

8.5.3. Voiceless Aspirated Palatal Plosive, /c^h/

Articulatory and Aerodynamic Description. The glottis is widely separated during and after the release of the palatal stricture. Consequently, no glottal oscillations are observed. The palatal contact is less tense than in /c/. There is a similar build-up of pressure, both in magnitude and manner, to that of /c/.

Acoustic Description. The mean duration of the stop phase is 85 ms after which the appearance of two spikes is common as in /ɟ/ and /c/. The frication and aspiration segments are readily noticeable. F_1 and F_2 values show no change from those of /c/ and /ɟ/.

8.6. *Voiceless (Unaspirated) Uvular Plosive, /q/*

Articulatory and Aerodynamic Description. The glottis is adducted during the greater part of the supraglottal occlusion. However, there are indications of slight opening in the initial phase of the occlusion. Vibration is inhibited because of myodynamic and aerodynamic conditions i. e., great muscular tension and high and sudden build-up of pressure. The stricture is located somewhere near the end of the oral cavity and just to the anterior of the pharyngeal cavity. It is executed by the extreme back of the tongue being raised and retracted so as to come into firm contact with the uvula. The upward movement of the tongue must be considerable otherwise it will be difficult to achieve a stricture with the uvula which simultaneously functions to block the nasal passage tightly. The nasal passage is certainly sealed off as no air seepage is detected during the occlusion. A corollary to this drastic upward gesture of the tongue, is the drastic elevation of the larynx. In fact, laryngeal elevation for /q/ exceeds that of all other sounds in the Koine.

Despite noticeable glottal constriction, the pressure is very high and it shoots up very quickly. There are three major factors that account for the high pressure: the small cavity behind the uvular stricture, the drastic larynx elevation and the tight velopharyngeal adduction.

The whole musculature of the vocal tract is extremely tense. The tenseness and the very high pressure account for the inhibition of voicing even though the glottis is constricted.

Acoustic Description. A well-defined transient marks the release of the occlusion which lasts for 99 ms. Voicing onset comes either with the release or is slightly delayed; thus the sound is unmistakenly unaspirated. The failure to recognize the absence of aspiration in /q/ may lead to its serious confusion with /k/. The confusion is most pertinent when NA or Arabic are taught as a foreign or second language. A high F_1 and a low F_2 are most characteristic of /q/; their values are in the range of 600–650 Hz and 1200–1300 Hz, respectively.

8.7. *Glottal Plosive (Stop), /ʔ/*

Articulatory and Aerodynamic Description. The tongue does not participate in the execution of the stricture. It is usually produced by completely closing the glottis to build up pressure which is suddenly relieved with the rapid separation of the vocal folds. However, there are cases when the approximation of the folds does not lead to a complete occlusion. This is consistent with Ladefoged's (1971:18) statement that: a glottal stop may have several degrees of tightness. When the glottis lacks the tight occlusion, /ʔ/ has vowel-like nature but the vibration is of the sort typical of creaky voice. Due to the location of /ʔ/ and the manner of its articulation, it is difficult, sometimes, to describe the sound as voiced or voiceless; nevertheless, vibration is immediately resumed in the following vowel. The body of the tongue is kept down at the floor of the mouth with its tip touching the lower incisors.

Acoustic Description. When the sound is the result of a complete occlusion at the glottis, it appears in the form of a blank column with a mean duration of 102 ms. The transient is hardly noticeable because the explosion which produces the sound is of low intensity. If the occlusion is relatively lax, the vocal folds are susceptible to vibration and the appearance of a few striations indicating creaky voice are not unusual. Only rarely does one observe a short delay of voicing in the following vowel. /ʔ/ seems to exert no influence on the formants of the adjacent vowels; on the contrary, its formant pattern represents that of the adjacent vowel.

8.8. Palato-Alveolar Affricates

/ǰ/ = Voiced Palato-Alveolar Affricate
/č/ = Voiceless Unaspirated Palato-Alveolar Affricate
/čh/ = Voiceless Aspirated Palato-Alveolar Affricate

8.8.1. Voiced Palato-Alveolar Affricate, /ǰ/

Articulatory and Aerodynamic Description. The glottis is adducted and vibration is maintained throughout the sound. As in all the voiced sounds, vibration becomes weaker towards the end, and sometimes it completely disappears just before the release. Even when vibration is maintained during the fricative segment, it is obscured by the turbulence noise at the supraglottal stricture. The contact is made as the body of the tongue moves forward and allows the tip-blade to touch the alveolar ridge somewhat less firmly than for its unaspirated counterpart. The tip-blade slides back under the influence of the anterior part of the palatine dorsum which must approach the hard palate to perform the necessary stricture for the fricative portion of /ǰ/. The initial complete occlusion followed by the narrow constriction interrupts the airstream causing a build-up of pressure; the build-up is, however, slow and low due to glottal impedance. The lips move from a neutral position to assume a slightly protruded and rounded shape.

Acoustic Description. The sound appears in the form of an initial stop with a mean duration of 69 ms. Voicing is indicated by the voice bar at the baseline. The stop is released gently and is immediately followed by moderate frication with feeble striations at the background. The mean duration of the fricative segment is only 40 ms. In general, voicing at the baseline of the fricative portion becomes very weak and sometimes it is barely noticeable. F_1 is usually very low throughout the sound but F_2 shows a noticeable excursion; it starts at about 1700 Hz for the stop segment then rises to about 2000 Hz for the fricative segment.

8.8.2. Voiceless Unaspirated Palato-Alveolar Affricate, /č/

Articulatory and Aerodynamic Description. The glottis is only slightly abducted during both the stop and the fricative phases. The sound is the result of an overall tense articulation which prolongs the stop phase. The constricted glottis seems to reduce the volume of airflow. With low airflow and tense glottis, turbulence noise is reduced both at the transition from the stop to the fricative phase and during the fricative phase. The overall difference between /č/ and its aspirated counterpart is in the amount of turbulence noise and the duration of the stop and fricative segments; they are 94 ms and 51 ms for /č/ and 72 ms and 91 ms for /čʰ/, respectively.[2]

Acoustic Description. The complete occlusion during the stop phase results in a silence gap with a mean duration of 94 ms which is followed by a weak transient indicating the release of the occlusion. Despite the weakness of the transient, it is still better defined than in /čʰ/. After the release, weak frication is observed which soon increases in intensity. F_1 and F_2 values are within the same range of those for /ǰ/.

8.8.3. Voiceless Aspirated Palato-Alveolar Affricate, /čʰ/

Articulatory and Aerodynamic Description. The glottis is abducted and allows a high rate of airflow thus providing good conditions for turbulence noise. Vibration almost disappears with the closing gesture of the supraglottal stricture due to the rapidly opening glottis. It is less tensely articulated than /č/ thus, expectedly, it has a shorter stop segment. But the higher rate of airflow leads to a longer fricative segment than for /č/.

Acoustic Description. The stop and the fricative phases are quite distinct and their mean durations are 72 ms and 91 ms, respectively, and they are in the reversed order of length compared with those of /č/. The transition between the two phases

---

2 For further phonetic and phonological details about the difference between them see Odisho, 1977a.

is less well-defined than in /č/, a feature that is associated with the less abrupt release of the stop element and the more convenient aerodynamic conditions for the generation of turbulence noise at the release of the stop phase and after it.

8.9. Alveolar Fricatives

/s/ = Voiceless Alveolar Fricative
/z/ = Voiced Alveolar Fricative

8.9.1. Voiceless Alveolar Fricative, /s/

Articulatory and Aerodynamic Description. The glottis is too wide to allow any vibration. The body of the tongue is pushed forward to enable the blade to execute the required stricture by coming very near to the alveolar ridge while the tip slightly touches the upper part of the lower incisors. The pressure is not as high as for its plosive cognates /t/ and /t^h/ due to the continuous seepage through the narrow slit at the alveolar region. The groove in the center of the blade which is repeatedly reported as a characteristic feature of /s/ in terms of general phonetics (Pike, 1966; Abercrombie, 1967; Gimson, 1967; Ladefoged, 1982) has been observed here, too. The air runs forcefully through the narrow constriction and hits against the incisors creating a very strong turbulence noise that is characteristic of all sibilant sounds.

Acoustic Description. The turbulence noise generated at the alveolar region is represented in the form of intense energy with a mean duration of 136 ms. The concentration of spectral energy is above 3500 Hz; it also exists, though with less intensity, below this level and above it up to 8000 Hz. Another typical acoustic feature of /s/–in fact of all the voiceless fricatives–is an aspirative segment with a duration of about 20–30 ms between the end of the frication and the onset of voice in the following vowel. This probably correlates with the movement of the vocal folds from a more open position during /s/ into a less open position for the subsequent vowel. F_1 and F_2 values are within the normal range for a stricture in the alveolar region; they are 250 Hz and 1800 Hz, respectively. There is a relatively sudden build-up of pressure which is much higher than in /z/.

8.9.2. Voiced Alveolar Fricative, /z/

Articulatory and Aerodynamic Description. The glottis is adducted and the vocal folds are in a state of vibration which is more evident in the first half of the stricture as the pressure drop across the glottis is still appropriate for proper vibration. The gradual build-up of pressure makes the aerodynamic conditions less favorable for vibration; however, vibration still persists during the second half of /z/ but noise also becomes evident. It is quite natural to observe less intense noise than in /s/ due to glottal impedance. Pressure build-up is very slow and is much lower than for its voiceless counterpart.

Acoustic Description. Noise and voice are maintained concurrently throughout the stricture for a mean duration of 101 ms. During the first half of the stricture noise is less intense and voice striations are more evident. The clarity of the voice striations and the noise is reversed in the second half. Spectral energy is concentrated above 3000–3500 Hz. F_1 is clearly displayed at the baseline while F_2, extrapolated from the adjacent formant transitions, is about 1800 Hz.

8.10. Palato-Alveolar Fricatives

/š/ = Voiceless Palato-Alveolar Fricative
/ž/ = Voiced Palato-Alveolar Fricative

8.10.1. Voiceless Palato-Alveolar Fricative, /š/

Articulatory and Aerodynamic Description. The glottis is open throughout the whole duration of the sound. The stricture is executed by elevating the anterior part of the palatine dorsum towards the hard palate while the tip-blade is approximated in the direction of the alveolar ridge. Consequently, the stricture is rather long though the significant constriction seems to be between the palatine dorsum and the anterior first third of the hard palate. Such a stricture is convenient for turbulence noise generation. Due to the continuous flow of air across the stricture, only medium pressure is built up. The lips are somewhat rounded and protruded.

Acoustic Description. The spectral energy, which represents the noise, fills the region between 2500 Hz and 8000 Hz with an average duration of 128 ms although it is less intense in the upper frequencies than in /s/. As with /s/, /š/ also has a short aspirative segment before the onset of voicing in the following vowel. F_1 and F_2 are in the range of 250 Hz and 2000–2200 Hz, respectively.

8.10.2. Voiced Palato-Alveolar Fricative, /ž/

Articulatory and Aerodynamic Description. The glottis is adducted and the vocal folds vibration is maintained throughout the whole duration of the stricture. Usually vibration becomes weaker towards the end of the sound. This is due to the gradual build-up of pressure which minimizes the pressure drop across the glottis and creates less favorable aerodynamic conditions for the maintenance of vibration. There is only a small build-up of pressure due to glottal impedance. Lip position is identical with that of /š/.

Acoustic Description. The mean duration of the sound is 108 ms which is usually a mixture of voice and noise. Voicing can easily be seen in the form of striations together with a voice bar at the baseline. The striations are more distinct in the first half of the segment.

8.11. *Uvular Fricatives*

/x/ = Voiceless Uvular Fricative
/ġ/ = Voiced Uvular Fricative

8.11.1. Voiceless Uvular Fricative, /x/

Articulatory and Aerodynamic Description. The glottis is abducted and the back of the tongue is raised towards the uvula behind which a relatively high pressure is built up. Although the uvula is raised to block the nasal passage like in any unnasalized or non-nasal sound, the lower surface of it dangles down to touch the raised part of the tongue. The high rate of airflow, due to open glottis, is forced through the uvular stricture. The result is not only the generation of turbulence noise but also the trilling of the uvula. There are 3–4 trills during each occurrence of /x/.

Acoustic Description. The absence of vibration is indicated by the absence of any voice striations. Instead the segment, with a duration of 114 ms, is filled with noise that starts at the level of F_2 up to 8000 Hz. The noise is more intense at formant level. Three or four well-defined striation-like vertical lines clearly appear within the segment; these "striations" represent the uvular trills which are at a distance of 20–30 ms from each other. The spectrogram of /x/ displays an F-pattern-like despite the unvoiced nature of the sound. This is explained in terms of the intensification of noise at formant level and its attenuation between them.

The levels of F_1 and F_2 at 600–650 Hz and 1400–1500 Hz, respectively, is reminiscent of /q/ and a good indication of their uvular nature rather than velar.

8.11.2. Voiced Uvular Fricative, /g̊/

Articulatory and Aerodynamic Description. The glottis is adducted and the vocal folds vibrate. The location of the stricture is identical with that of /x/. Glottal impedance allows smaller rates of airflow than for /x/; consequently, there is a low and slow build-up of pressure. No uvular trills are observed with /g̊/, a fact that is attributed to the lower rate of airflow across the stricture.

Acoustic Description. /g̊/ appears as a segment with a mixture of noise and voice. The striations stand for voicing and are evident throughout the whole duration of the sound. Noise is less intense than in /x/ and is mainly concentrated above 4000 Hz. The very weak noise accentuates the harmonics thus allowing a fairly clear F-pattern-like.

8.12. *Voiceless Glottal Fricative, /h/*

Articulatory and Aerodynamic Description. There is no significant impedance in the way of the airstream as the glottis is wide open; however, in intervocalic position weak vibration is likely not because of proper approximation of the vocal folds but because of the high rate of airflow which is typical of /h/ sounds, the voiceless fricatives and the voiceless aspirated plosives. The rate of airflow is sufficient to produce turbulence noise at the glottis and the vocal tract as a whole. This is probably why Strevens (1967:209) states that the area of turbulence noise for /h/ is very extensive. The anterior half of the tongue lies on the floor of the mouth with the tip touching the lower incisors. /h/ sounds have no specific tongue configurations and thus they are greatly influenced by the configuration of the adjacent vowels.

Acoustic Description. /h/ appears in the form of random low intensity noise above 1500 Hz up to 5500 Hz the duration of which is 100–130 ms. Noise is more visible at the level of F_2 and F_3. However, since the articulation of /h/ does not bring about a radical deformation of the vocal tract configuration, noise concentration is determined by the vocal tract specifications of the adjacent sounds, specifically the vowels. /h/ is one of the sounds the duration of which is difficult to measure due to its undefined boundaries.

8.13. Central Approximants

8.13.1. Labio-Palatal Approximant, /ɥ/

Articulatory and Aerodynamic Description. The glottis is adducted and vocal folds vibrate. The center of the tongue is raised towards the region between the hard and the soft palate. This entails that the stricture is relatively more advanced than for the labiovelar approximant [w]. Simultaneously, the lips are brought horizontally together then rounded and protruded. This feature is also more noticeable than in [w]. The open approximation stricture allows for an incessant flow of air capable of setting the vocal folds into action but incapable of causing any turbulence noise at the stricture. It is quite difficult for the phonetically untrained people to distinguish [ɥ] from [w].

Acoustic Description. Voicing is indicated at the level of F_1 and the upper formants 4 and 5. The excursion of F_2 out of /ɥ/ at 1500 Hz indicates that its level is not consistent with F_2 level in palatal sounds. Nevertheless, if the drastic lip-rounding is taken into consideration the relative lowness of the second formant will become more realistic as lip-rounding greatly depresses all the formants.

8.13.2. Palatal Approximant, /y/

Articulatory and Aerodynamic Description. The glottis is adducted and the vibration is maintained. The center of the tongue is raised so as to come into proximity with the hard palate and form a narrower stricture than that of vowel /i/. The tongue, however, does not seem to retain the same position in relation to the hard palate; it soon slides from its position in a manner consistent with the subsequent sound. This is what in phonetics is referred to as a glide i.e., a glide from one position to the other. There is only a low build-up of pressure due to glottal impedance. The continuous airflow which passes across the stricture very gently, hardly produces any turbulence. The lips assume a spread position quite contrary to the rounded lip position of /ɥ/.

Acoustic Description. It is rather difficult to pinpoint the boundaries of this sound because of its gliding nature and the vowel-like specifications. A rough estimation of its length will be in the range of 120–140 ms. The segment portrays a fairly visible F-pattern with well-defined striations in the background. The location of the stricture in the palatal region with no lip-rounding leads to a maximum separation of F_1 and F_2 and an approximation of F_2 and F_3.

8.14. Lateral Approximant, /l/

Articulatory and Aerodynamic Description. The left side of the palatine dorsum is depressed to allow an appropriate opening for /l/ production. The glottis is adducted and the vibration continues throughout the sound as the airflow freely runs mainly through the left-side opening with no friction at all. The tip of the tongue remains in contact with the alveolar ridge.

Acoustic Description. /l/ appears as a vowel-like segment with a distinct F-pattern and quite visible striations. Its mean duration is 110 ms. F_1 and F_2 values are typical of alveolar sounds. The absence of any noise is attributed to the wide lateral opening.

8.15. Nasal Approximants

8.15.1. Bilabial Nasal Approximant, /m/

Articulatory and Aerodynamic Description. The complete oral occlusion makes the sound eligible for classification as a stop, but the free passage of air through the nose converts the sound into a typical approximant. The glottis is adducted and vibration continues due to the continuous seepage through the nose.

Acoustic Description. As in all the approximants, one needs several cues to be able to delimit the sound. The sharp transitions into and out of a nasal sound and the noticeable difference in intensity are good cues for identifying nasal sounds. The F-pattern is not as clear-cut as in other approximants or vowels because of the damping influence of the nasal chamber and the resulting weakness in voicing. Both F_1 and F_2 are very low; the former is at the baseline while the latter is only 800–900 Hz high.

8.15.2. Alveolar Nasal Approximant, /n/

Articulatory and Aerodynamic Description. The glottis is adducted and the aerodynamic conditions are good for vibration though similar to /m/, vibration is weakened due to damping along the nasal passage. The tongue tip anchors between the upper incisors and the alveolar ridge and the uvula is depressed to provide a free passage for the airflow.

Acoustic Description. /n/ displays a somewhat more distinct F-pattern than that of /m/. There is also a distinct difference in the level of F_2 which for /n/ is 1600–1700 Hz.

8.16. *Alveolar Tap, /r/*

Articulatory and Aerodynamic Description. The vibration is maintained during the sound due to the adducted glottis and the absence of a long obstruction of the airflow due to the nature of a tap /r/. When this sound is produced in isolation, the tip of the tongue is raised swiftly from its neutral position and is slightly retracted and then suddenly thrown against the alveolar ridge to interrupt the airflow only temporarily. But when the sound occurs in a certain context, the place from which the tip moves to execute the tap, depends on the position of the tip for the sound preceding /r/. In most cases, the excursion of the tongue tip produces a glide or a vowel-like element that comes just before the brief occlusion. The single-tap nature of /r/ in the Koine is the most dominant realization, but in the case of gemination the sound is realized as a trill simply because the tap is repeated more than once.

Acoustic Description. The main acoustic feature of /r/ that is readily observed is the silence gap with a mean duration of about 30 ms. The gap stands for the rapid occlusion that is preceded by a couple of voice striations representing the glide of the tongue tip. Voicing is easily detected by the voice bar at the baseline while F_2 is at about 1400 Hz.

CHAPTER IX

A PHONETIC DESCRIPTION OF EMPHASIS

9.1. *Introductory Remarks*

In the phonology part of this book emphasis was treated as a long component the features of which spread beyond the limits of a single segment. For convenience the features were associated with the word. Consequently, words were identified as either having emphasis or not having it. Such a phonological solution should not mean that the piece which is assigned the feature of "+ emphatic" has the phonetic exponents of emphasis at every point within its boundary. It should be made clear, at this juncture, that a piece is marked emphatic either on the basis of the full realization of the features of emphasis or by implication. Implication is used here to cover all those words for which the features of emphasis are found in most parts of a word but not necessarily in all parts of it. Notice that in

+/tura/ "mountain," +/turan/ "our mountain" and +/turoxun/ "your mountain"

the first two pieces are fully emphaticized whereas the third one is only partially emphaticized as the features of emphasis taper off on its final syllable. In other words the last piece is granted an emphatic status by implication. This treatment is quite practical as a phonological device because if the above pieces are compared with the ones below, which are all fully unemphatic, the contrast is maximized and sounds more justifiable:

/t^{h}ura/ "twig," /t^{h}uran/ "our twig" and /t^{h}uroxun/ "your twig".

It was also pointed out earlier on that all segments, both vocalic and consonantal, are susceptible to emphasis although the category of palatal consonants was singled out as less susceptible due to articulatory inconveniency. This, however, does not mean that the susceptible sounds expound the same features of emphasis, with the same clarity and to the same extent because emphasis is introduced here as a complex phenomenon involving several articulatory maneuvers. This implies that the articulatory maneuvers may differ from one category of sounds to the other. The distinctive role of each feature will be specified separately with each category but there is one significant feature that has been unanimously reported as indispensable for emphaticizing all sounds. The feature has been labelled differently, but in modern physiological terms it is known as *pharyngeal constriction*. It has been reported as early as 1948 when Marcias published a study on emphasis in Arabic supported by X-ray tracings. The tracings displayed the projection of the root of the tongue into the pharynx resulting in the reduction of its volume. Since then this feature has been taken for granted when dealing with emphasis. Some investigators (Al-Ani, 1970; Ali & Daniloff, 1972) have produced further experimental evidence to confirm the pharyngeal constriction and elaborate on other articulatory aspects of emphasis.

Occasionally, pharyngeal constriction has been regarded so important that emphasis has been labelled "pharyngealization" (Abercrombie, 1967). Obviously this is an inaccurate identification. For a more accurate and realistic identification of emphasis other features have to be taken into consideration. Flattening or depression of the anterior part of the tongue has been observed and reported (Mitchell, 1956, 1969; Al-Ani, 1970; Ali & Daniloff, 1972; Odisho, 1973). For coronal sounds–sounds for which the anterior portion of the tongue is the active articulator (Chomsky & Halle, 1968)–the depression leads to concavity. Lip protrusion and rounding have also been reported as relevant factors in emphasis (Blanc, 1953; Mitchell, 1956; Jakobson, 1957; Lehn, 1963; El-Haleese, 1971; Gaber, 1972). Our investigation has shown that laryngeal elevation could be a significant feature in emphaticizing the coronal sound, in particular (Odisho, 1975). Besides, the tense articulation of emphatic sounds as opposed to the lax articulation of their unemphatic counterparts constitutes a difference of prime importance.

As for the study of emphasis in NA no investigation of the underlying mechanism is, hitherto, reported. This scarcity of information justifies the next sections in this chapter.

9.2. *Consonants in Emphatic Contexts*

9.2.1. Bilabials

These sounds being non-coronal, the tip of the tongue is not involved in performing their primary stricture, therefore, tongue depression or concavity is not likely; instead it is more spread and retracted to bring about the pharyngeal constriction. Another noticeable feature of emphatic bilabials is the behavior of the cheeks and the lips; the former are blown out and the latter are relatively protruded. Acoustically, F_1 is slightly raised and F_2 is lowered as a result of the change in the volumes of the front and back cavities. Obviously, F_2 is originally low for the bilabials, but here it is further lowered.

9.2.2. Alveolars

All these sounds are coronal and require the tip or the blade to move forward to execute the primary stricture. As the back of the tongue is required to drift backwards towards the posterior pharyngeal wall, the tongue undergoes two antagonistic maneuvers which are the main reason behind tongue flattening and the depression of the palatine dorsum. The need to maintain two strictures simultaneously forces the whole laryngeal structure to move upwards. Due to this fact laryngeal elevation is more noticeable with alveolars than with the rest of the consonants. The acoustic outcome of the above articulatory maneuvers is a noticeable rise in F_1 and a considerable lowering in F_2 creating great proximity between F_1 and F_2, a feature so characteristic of alveolar emphatics. The pharyngeal constriction, tongue depression or concavity and lip-rounding all jointly contribute in creating the proximity.

9.2.3. Palatals

From the articulatory point-of-view, the palatals are the result of an almost horizontal contact vector between the active and passive articulators. Such a type of stricture makes the retention of an appropriate contact rather difficult if the back of the tongue is allowed to make an adequate rearward movement into the pharyngeal cavity to perform the secondary stricture. It is, therefore, thought that in order to maintain the required primary stricture, which is basic for the retention of the identity of the palatals, the tongue backing gesture does not take its full range as in the case of the alveolars and bilabials. In other words the backing gesture is not ideally realized due to the lack of proper anchorage for the retention of the primary stricture. This anchorage hypothesis is the perspective in terms of which the incompatibility of palatals with emphasis is explained. This fact could probably provide an explanation for the shift in the place of articulation of /ɥ/ and [č]=[tš] from palatal to velar and alveolar, respectively, i. e., they become [w] and [tṣ]. With [w], the more retracted location provides better features of emphasis, while with [tṣ] the alveolar location provides a better anchorage to allow more freedom for the retraction of the back of the tongue. It also explains the fact that emphasis in the Semitic languages is essentially associated with alveolar and dental sounds.

Because of the limited backing gesture, only little downward displacement of F_2 is observed, F_1 shows less upward movement.

9.2.4. Uvulars

They are non-coronal sounds with their primary stricture already in the pharyngeal region. The anterior half of the tongue being free provides a leeway for further pharyngeal constriction. The additional constriction is easily felt by the speaker. The palatine dorsum is pressed to the floor of the oral cavity and the lips are increased in rounding. The salient acoustic feature of plain uvulars is a high F_1 and a moderately low F_2. In other words, the two formants are fairly close to each other. With emphasis the proximity is increased; therefore, F_1 and F_2 appear like a single dark band very similar to that of the alveolars and bilabials.

9.3. *Vowels in Emphatic Contexts*

The vowels are also relatively different in their compatibility with emphasis according to their degree of frontness/backness, openness/closeness and lip position. Unlike the consonants, the anchorage requirement does not arise here since vowels have an open approximation stricture. This entails that vowels, in general, should maintain a fair degree of compatibility with emphasis and their basic configuration is easily affected by the backing gesture. The change in the shape of the tongue alters the cavity volumes thus yielding different F-patterns.

In the following sections a comparative description of vowels in plain and emphatic contexts is made. The description is basically in acoustic terms.

9.3.1. /i/ vs. +/i/

In /i/ F_1 and F_2 are estimated at about 250 Hz and 2200 Hz, whereas in +/i/ F_1 value ranges from 350 Hz at the onset down to 250 Hz at the offset and F_2 ranges from 1250 Hz at the onset up to about 2000 Hz at the offset. This means that the quality of the vowel is not constant. And if F_1 is taken to represent openness and F_2 frontness, +/i/ is relatively more open than /i/ and is considerably retracted. So at least in the first portion of +/i/ the quality of the vowel changes rather greatly as a result of centralization. Only towards the end the vowel manages to regain its steady-state quality similar to that of /i/.

9.3.2. /ɪ/ vs. +/ɪ/

F_1 and F_2 in /ɪ/ are 350 Hz and 1800 Hz and in +/ɪ/ they become 450 Hz and 1250 Hz, respectively. Thus /ɪ/ has already a relatively centralized quality. With +/ɪ/ the centralization is more noticeable; in fact, it becomes almost identical with a schwa.

9.3.3. /e/ vs. +/e/

/e/ is a mid vowel with values of 500 Hz and 1900 Hz for F_1 and F_2, respectively. In +/e/ formant values, like those of +/i/, are not constant. At the onset F_1 starts at about 600 Hz and descends down to 500 Hz and F_2 starts at 1000 Hz and ascends up to about 1900 Hz. As expected, +/e/ is lowered and considerably retracted at least throughout its first half. The quality of +/e/ is similar to the British English vowel in words like "girl" and "serve."

9.3.4. /a/ vs. +/a/

The stricture for /a/ is located toward the back of the oral cavity thus dividing the vocal tract into a small back cavity and a large front one and yielding a rather high F_1 at about 700 Hz and a medium F_2 at about 1400 Hz. With +/a/ the volume of the back cavity is decreased even further by additional pharyngeal constriction, therefore, F_1 and F_2 value become 800 Hz and 1100 Hz, respectively. However, the formant excursion in +/a/ is not as great as in +/i/ and +/e/ because the additional pharyngeal constriction is limited. Nevertheless, +/a/ is unmistakenly retracted and lowered; its short variant is identical with the British English vowel as in "but" and "shut" while its long variant is identical with Cardinal Vowel No. 5 or the British English vowel as in "father" and "guard."

9.3.5. /o/ vs. +/o/

/o/ is a back rounded vowel. It is known that lip rounding usually lowers the formants, in particular F_2 which is expectedly at 1150 Hz. F_1 at 500 Hz is still relatively high despite the lip rounding, because of the back location of the primary stricture. In +/o/, F_1 and F_2 values become 650 Hz and 1000 Hz indicating only a limited change in vowel quality.

9.3.6. /u/ vs. +/u/

The back and the rounded nature of /u/ enable the vowel to resist drastic qualitative change as the above two features already represent qualities that are consistent with emphasis. The qualitative difference between /u/ and +/u/ is less than in all vowels in the Koine. Both lowering and retraction are less conspicuous in this instance. F_1 at 250 Hz for /u/, is much lower than for /o/. The difference could be associated with maximum rounding in the case of the former. F_2 is at 950 Hz. The limited qualitative change is inferred from the values of F_1 and F_2 for +/u/ which are 300 Hz and 850 Hz, respectively.

9.4. Concluding Remarks

To recapitulate, the front spread and unrounded vowels /i, ɪ, e, a/ seem to be more susceptible to the influence of emphasis than the back rounded vowels. However, it is pertinent to point out that the limited difference in the efficiency of displaying the features of emphasis hardly affects the distinguishability of the plain and emphatic versions of the back rounded vowels due to the fact that in speech the phenomenon of emphasis is not restricted to single segments. Emphasis is a long feature whose auditory impact on the listener is assessed on the basis of the overall contribution of all the segments in the word rather than on the basis of the separate contribution of each single segment.

CHAPTER X

A PHONETIC DESCRIPTION OF DOUBLE PLOSIVE CLUSTERS

10.1. *Introductory Remarks*

Although clusters in the Koine are confined to the initial position only and are not larger in size in the stem than two elements, the dialect is still regarded as relatively rich in cluster formations. An examination of all cluster varieties is not of great phonetic interest since most of the varieties are attested in other languages. However, a few comments on /p^h, t^h, c^h/ plus /r/ clusters, before dealing with the main theme, are necessary due to the tap nature of /r/ in the Koine.

It has been reported for English (Gimson, 1967; Klatt, 1973) that when the voiceless plosives form clusters with the sonorants (approximants) /w, y, m, n, l, r/, the sonorants are devoiced. Thus in the phonetic transcription of such clusters the aspiration mark is deleted and the devoicing mark is placed under the sonorants, e. g., /p^h + r/ > [p$\r{r}$]. This is a typical case of coarticulation in which the glottal abduction posture for the plosives is extended into the domain of the approximants.

The devoicing phenomenon applies to all such clusters in the Koine except when an /r/ is involved. There is only one way to account for this exception. The tap nature of /r/, i. e., [ɾ] which is dominant in most NA dialects, seems to create less favorable articulatory and aerodynamic conditions for devoicing than the sonorant (approximant) /r/ in English. It may, however, be devoiced occasionally when in combination with a /t^h/ that is heavily aspirated.

The only significant conclusion from the above comments is the fact that not all the sounds represented by the symbol "r" or any other equivalent symbol in other languages are identical. r's could be immensely different from the articulatory point-of-view. A corollary to this difference is the diversified aerodynamic conditions and hence dissimilar acoustic features. This is, therefore, the rationale for transcribing those clusters, even phonetically, as [p^hr, t^hr, c^hr] rather than [p$\r{r}$, t$\r{r}$, c$\r{r}$].

The most characteristic clusters in the Koine are the *plosive plus plosive* ones also known as *double-plosive* clusters. Few languages have this kind of clusters especially in the initial position. Besides, literature on the phonetic formation and features of double-plosive clusters is very rare. The above two reasons have motivated the devotion of this chapter to a detailed investigation of this aspect of the Koine.

10.2. Double-Plosive Clusters

The Koine displays a wide variety of double-plosive clusters. Their formation is subject to a stringent constraint which is more associated with the glottal stricture and activity rather than with the place of articulation. Glottal stricture and activity have already yielded a trichotomy of single plosives known as voiced, voiceless unaspirated and voiceless aspirated. In cluster formation, those three opposing features are almost always mutually exclusive in that both members of the cluster have either to be voiced, voiceless unaspirated or voiceless aspirated. They are, henceforth, known as voiced, unaspirated and aspirated, respectively.

The following clusters /bd/, /ɟd/, /pt/, /pc/, /tʰpʰ/, /pʰtʰ/, were investigated in the contexts of the words /bdaya/ "breaking a promise", /ɟdala/ "thread," /ptamɪr/, "will say," /pcartɪn/ "will curl," /tʰpʰana/ "becoming mouldy" and /pʰtʰaya/ "becoming wide." Five tokens of each cluster were produced.

10.2.1. Articulatory and Aerodynamic Observations

The general pattern of the pressure traces for almost all clusters is a double-peaked one, i.e., there is a dip in the middle of the pressure pulse. Occasionally, the dip disappears such as in the case of /pc/. When this happens, there is a continuous rise in pressure until the second plosive is released. The first peak is usually lower than the second one except in /tʰpʰ/ for which either the two peaks are almost equal or the first peak is only slightly higher. To give the reader an idea about the pressure patterns, the traces of the first three tokens are found below superimposed on each other. (Fig. 10) The superimposition of two more traces was avoided lest it should obscure the overall pressure traces as they were very similar to the first three.

As for the glottal strictures of those clusters, the voiceless aspirated have a wide open glottis almost throughout the whole cluster and for a while after it. There seems to be one unified opening gesture for both members of the cluster. The voiceless unaspirated show some initial abduction of the glottis in the initial phase of the first plosive which ends up in what seems to be complete adduction throughout the rest of the cluster duration. For both the aspirated and unaspi-

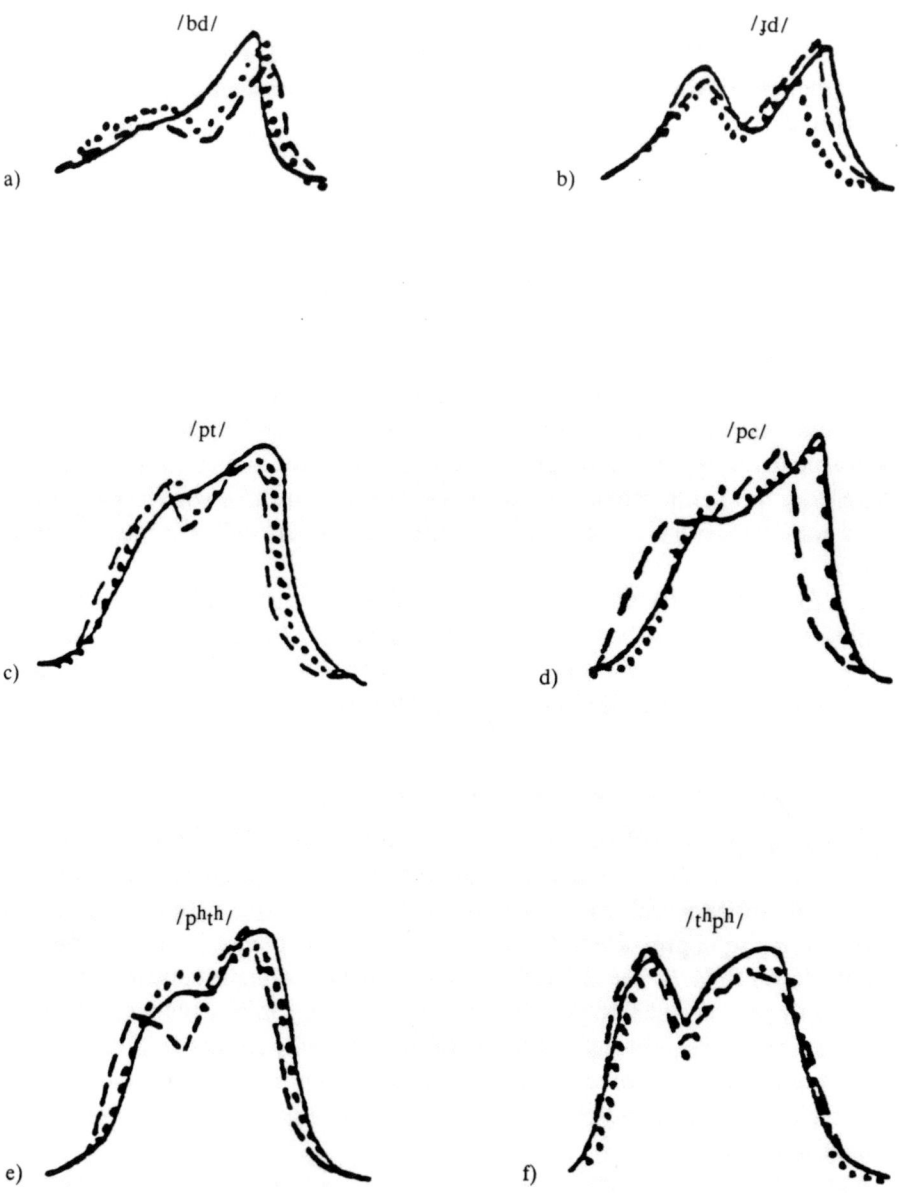

Fig. 10 a, b, c, d, e, f. Pressure patterns for /bd/, /ɟd/, /pt/, /pc/, $p^h t^h$/ and $t^h p^h$/. In each case three patterns, traced from real tokens, are superimposed on each other.

rated clusters, limited vibration at their onset is observed which soon disappears. The glottis is adducted for the voiced clusters and vibration is maintained throughout the supraglottal stricture.

10.2.2. Acoustic Observations

There is a distinct clear voice-bar at the baseline of the voiced clusters. The other two categories of clusters have no voice-bars; only some voicing is detected at their onset which lasts a short duration of about 20–40 ms which represents the persistence of vibration from a vowel in the carrier (frame) sentence. All clusters show some spectral energy between the two components the width of which differs according to: (a) whether the cluster is aspirated, unaspirated or voiced; (b) whether the first element is a bilabial, alveolar or palatal.

10.3. *Discussion and Conclusions*

The members of each cluster seem to retain their main characteristics as in the form of single consonants. Voicing persistence for the aspirated and the unaspirated caused by the vowel preceding the cluster in the frame sentence dies out early enough during the first member of the cluster to leave the remaining part of the first plosive and the whole of the second plosive voiceless. For the unaspirated cluster, voicing is initiated just after the release of its second member yielding a very short VOT so typical of unaspirated plosives. Whereas the open glottis after the release of the second plosive in an aspirated cluster delays the voicing onset consequently leading to a large VOT value which is the most significant feature in realizing the aspirated plosives as well as the clusters. Voicing for the voiced clusters is continued throughout their whole duration.

The only difference between the cluster-plosive production and single-plosive production is the relatively shorter closure duration for the former than for the latter. The reduction in closure duration might be explained, as Scully put it, in terms of compression in time as much as possible in order, quite simply, to save time (Scully, 1973:6).

The domain of the spectral energy appearing after the release of the first member of, particularly, the aspirated cluster may be taken as a reliable technique to determine the frication duration as a different phenomenon from aspiration. This is based on the fact that since in those clusters we have a single glottal abduction gesture and since the glottis is too widely abducted at the time of the release of the first plosive for turbulence noise to be generated, therefore, the spectral energy observed between the two members of the clusters is taken to be the acoustic manifestation of the turbulence noise generated at the supraglottal stricture when the first plosive is released.

As for the pressure traces and their general double-peaked pattern, this depends mainly on the release of the first plosive which causes a dip in the middle of the pressure pulse. But the fact that the second peak is frequently higher than the first may be attributed to a relatively incomplete evacuation of the oral pressure after the release of the first plosive as the supraglottal closing gesture for the second one follows soon. In other words, by the time the supraglottal closing gesture for the second plosive starts causing a build-up in intraoral pressure there is already a fairly high background pressure. The extent of the height of the second peak may also depend on the potential intraoral pressure of the second plosive and the difference in the volume of the two cavities created behind the stricture of each member of the cluster. For instance, it is expected for the second peak to be higher in a voiceless aspirated cluster if the occurrence of the members of the cluster are in this order: /p^{h}t^h/ rather than in this order: /t^{h}p^h/. This is because the potential intraoral pressure for /t^h/ is higher than for /p^h/ (the mean peak pressure values for /t^h/ and p^h/ as single plosives being 9.9 cm H$_2$O and 7.3 cm H$_2$O, respectively) and also because in /p^{h}t^h/ cluster the shift is from a relatively large cavity to a smaller one. The occasional absence of the dip in the pressure trace of /pc/ cluster, despite the order of the cavity sizes, may be attributed to a different reason. Here the reason lies in the articulatory autonomy the organs or part of organs that are involved in the execution of each plosive enjoy. The lips for /p/ and the middle of the tongue for /c/ represent two independent systems which implies the possibility of executing the latter sound while the former is not released or at least the closing gesture of the second plosive is initiated with only a fractional delay. Apparently the latter situation is dominant with /pc/ which allows for a small pressure release that is capable of producing only a feeble acoustic signal between the plosives.

The above discussion seems to have significant bearing on issues in general phonetics and the enhancement of our awareness about the underlying mechanisms that produce our sounds and organize them in speech. The significance is associated with the following two points:

(a) In the Koine the double-plosive clusters rarely involve an incomplete plosion (i.e., not to release the first plosive). They are unlike the production of such clusters or two consecutive plosives in English. Their phonetic realization in the Koine is more similar so what exists in French where the closing gesture of the second plosive usually comes after the release gesture of the first plosive.

(b) The intervening segment that appears between the two elements of the aspirated clusters represents the burst and the frication domain of the first plosive, i.e., the aspiration period is almost missing. This naturally entails that for the unaspirated clusters the intervening element represents nothing but the burst only with minimum frication. In the voiced clusters it usually represents the burst which is occasionally coupled with a very short vowel-like element that fails to establish itself auditorily as an epenthetic vowel.

APPENDIX

GLOTTOGRAMS, PRESSURE TRACES AND SPECTROGRAMS

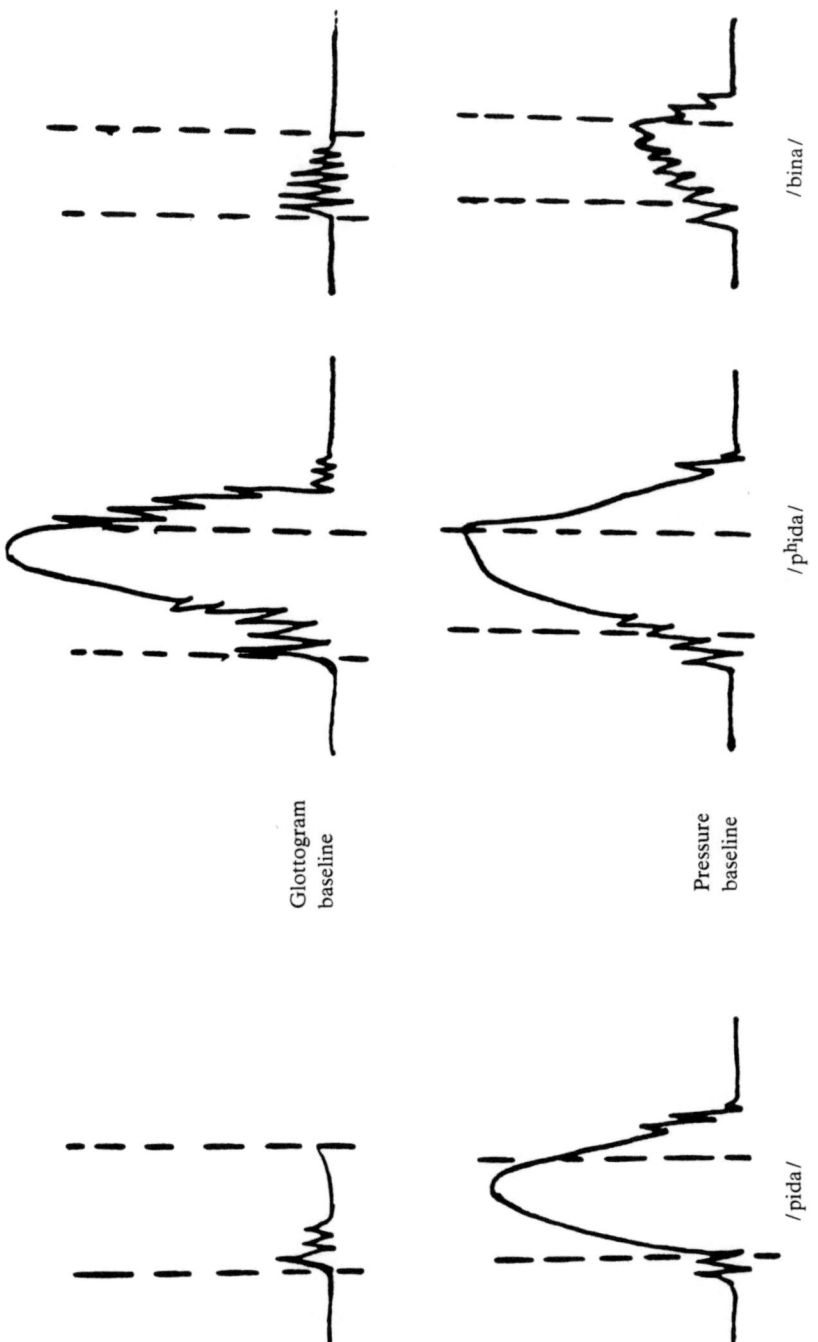

Fig. 11. Traces based on real tokens of a-glottograms (up), b-Intraoral pressure pulses (down) for /p/, /pʰ/ and /b/ in the contexts of /pida/, /pʰida/ and /bina/.

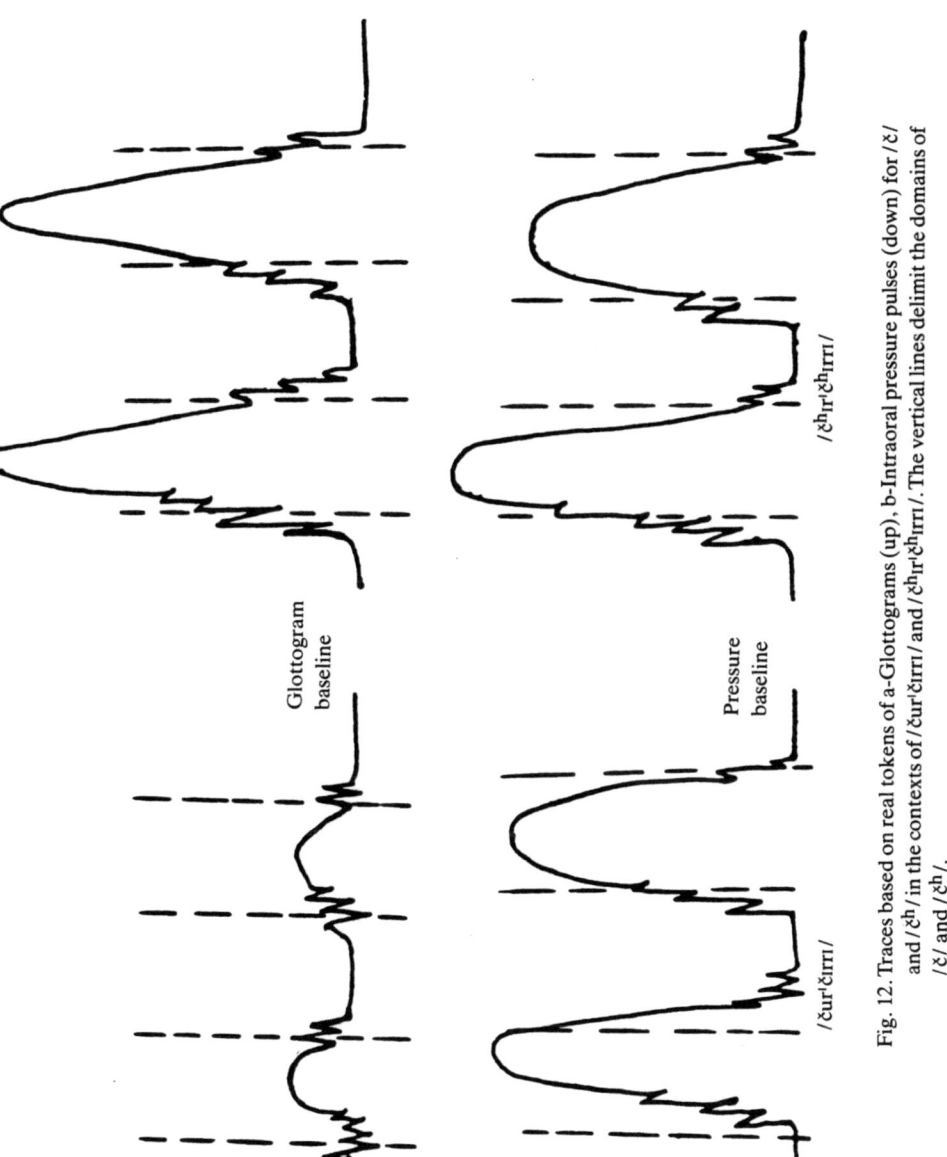

Fig. 12. Traces based on real tokens of a-Glottograms (up), b-Intraoral pressure pulses (down) for /č/ and /čʰ/ in the contexts of /čurˈčɪrrɪ/ and /čʰrˈčʰɪrrɪ/. The vertical lines delimit the domains of /č/ and /čʰ/.

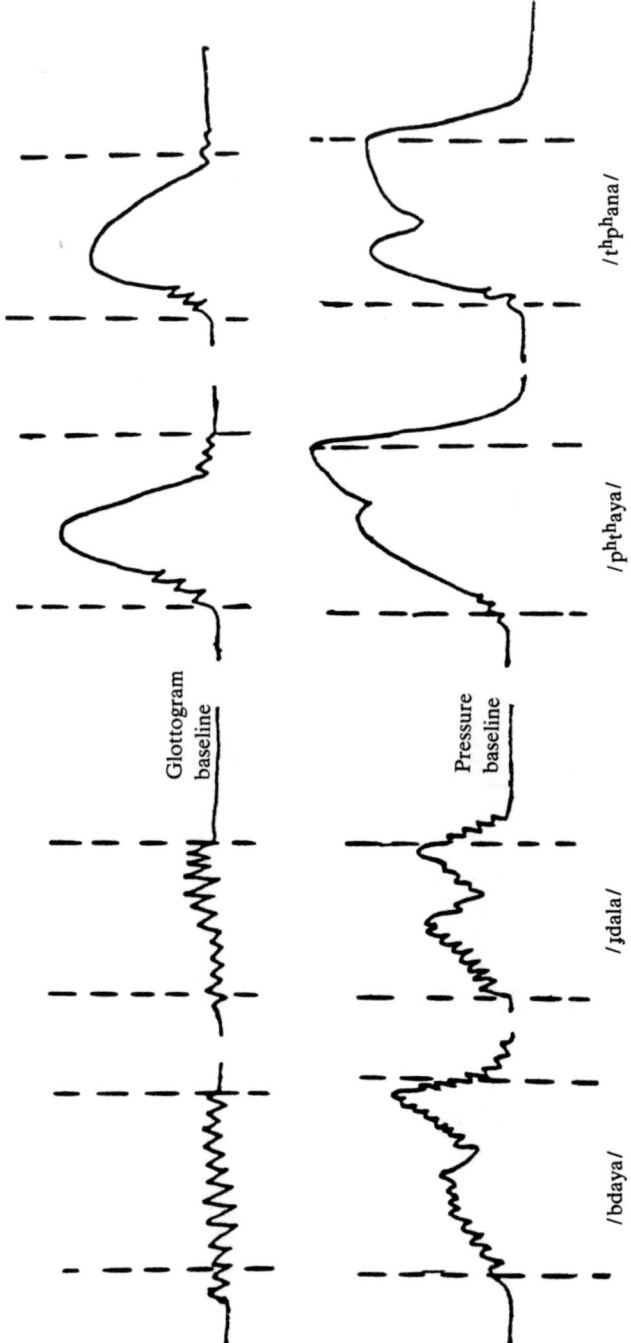

Fig. 13. Traces based on real tokens of a-Glottograms (up), b-Intraoral pressure pulses (down) for the clusters /bd/, /jd/, /p^{h}t^h/ and /t^{h}p^h/ in the contexts of /bdaya/, /jdala/, /p^{h}t^{h}aya/ and /t^{h}p^{h}ana/.

SPECTROGRAMS
1–19

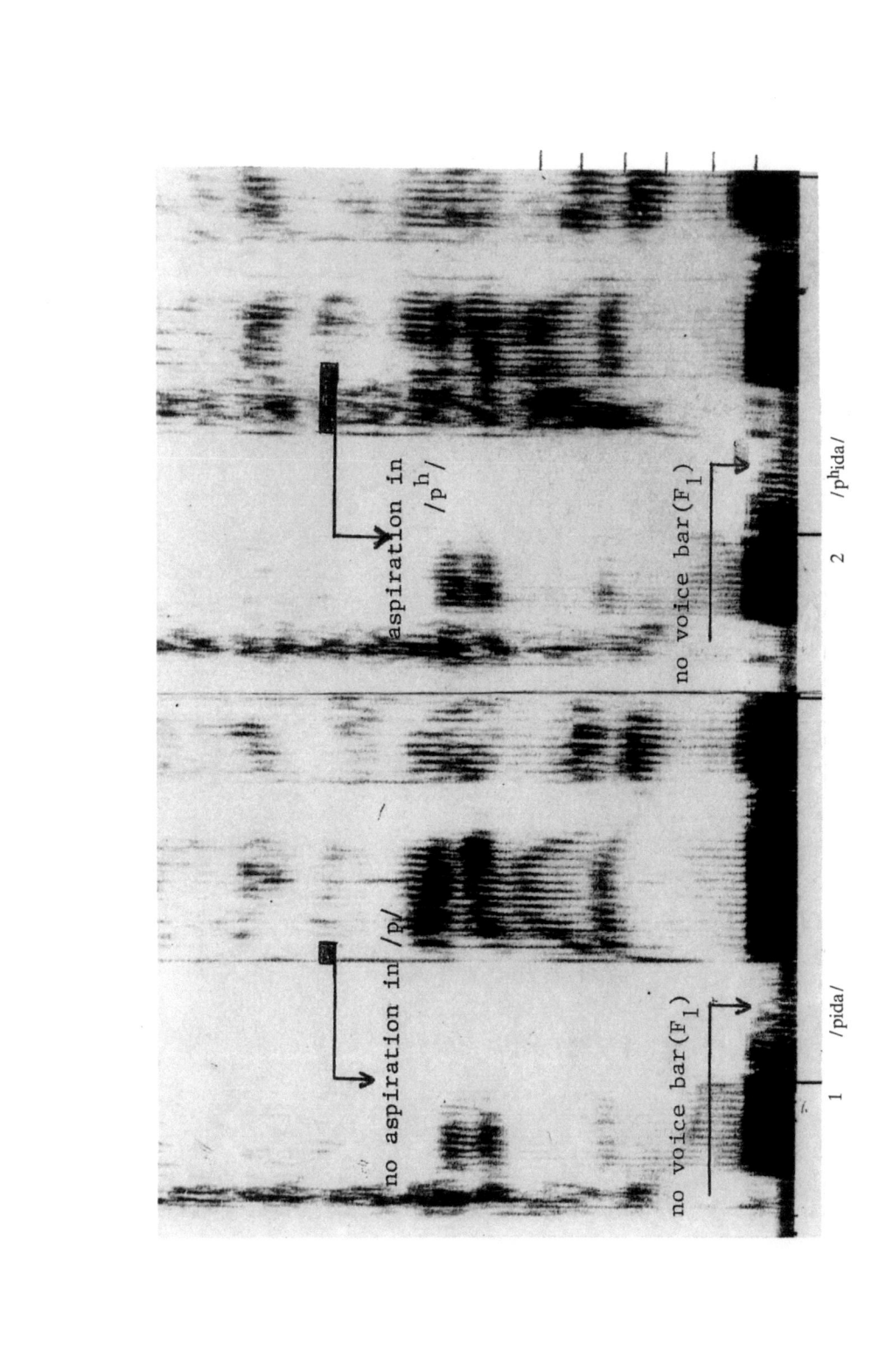

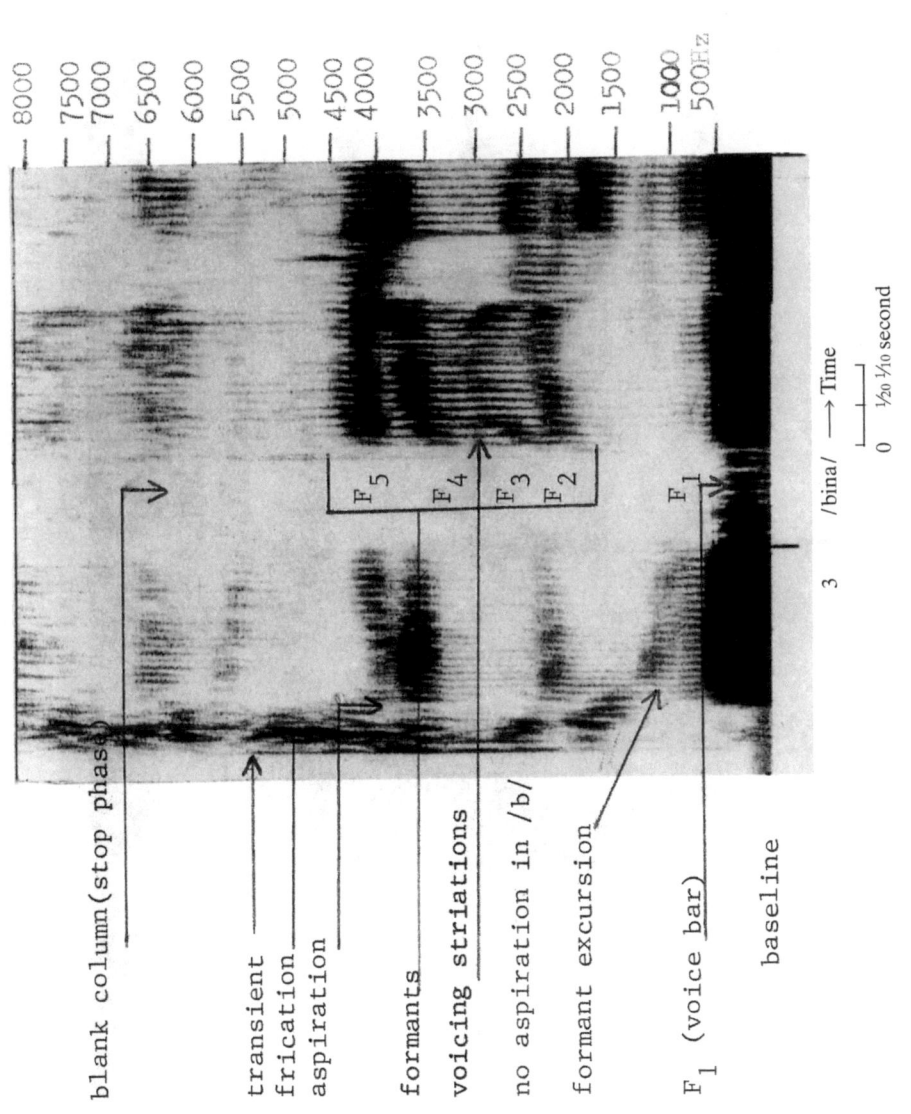

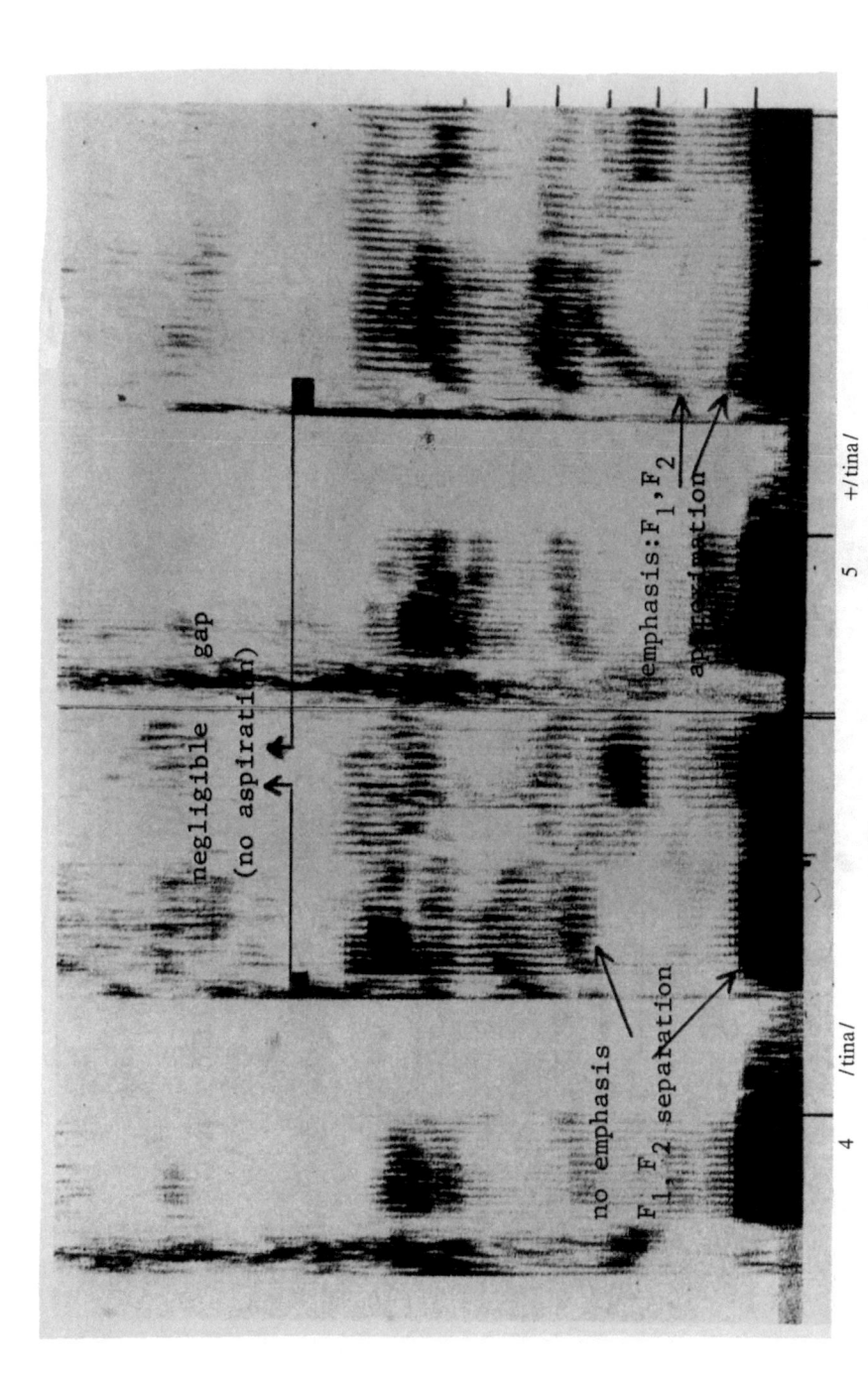

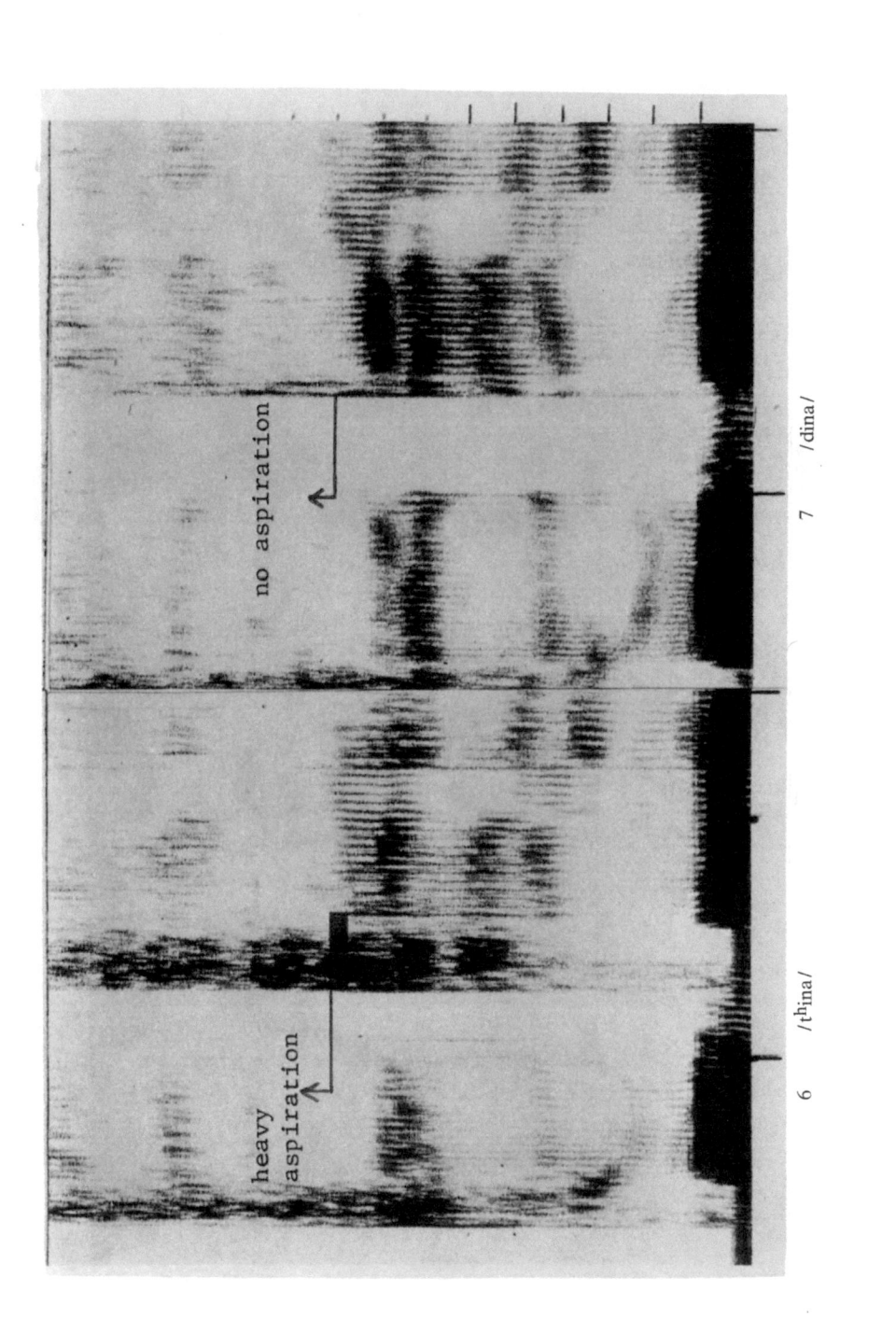

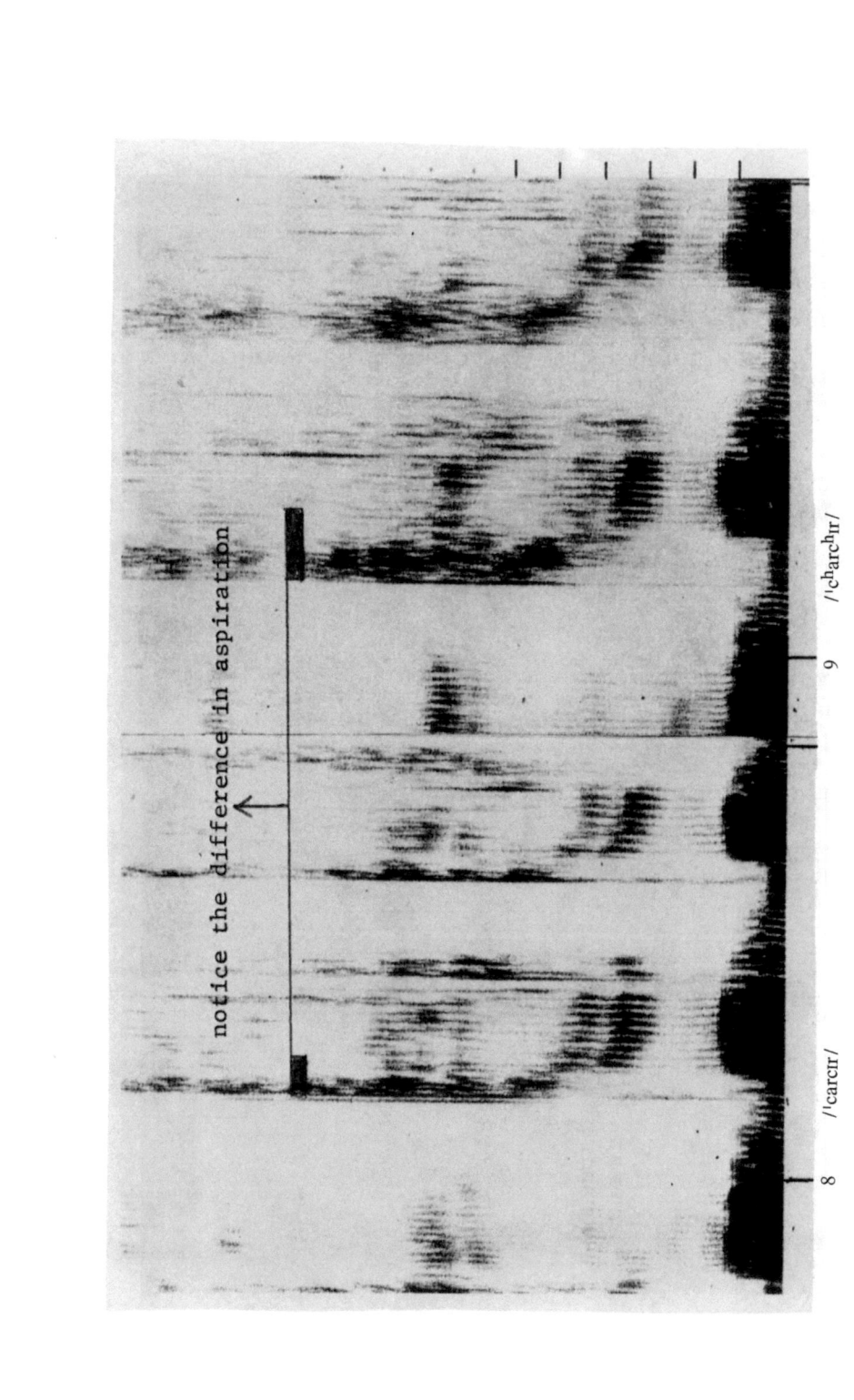

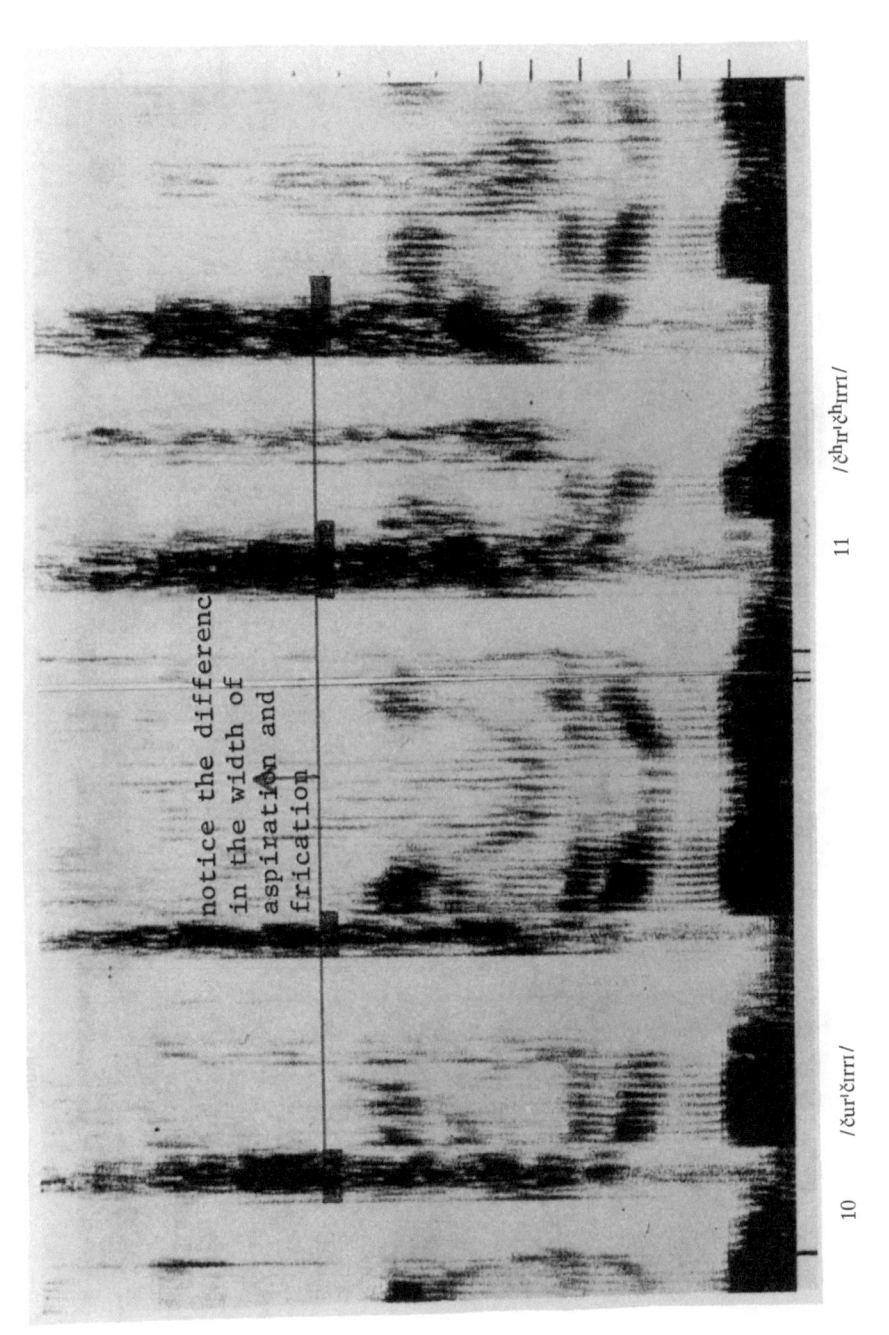

10 /čurˈčɪrrɪ/   11 /čhrɪčhɪrrɪ/

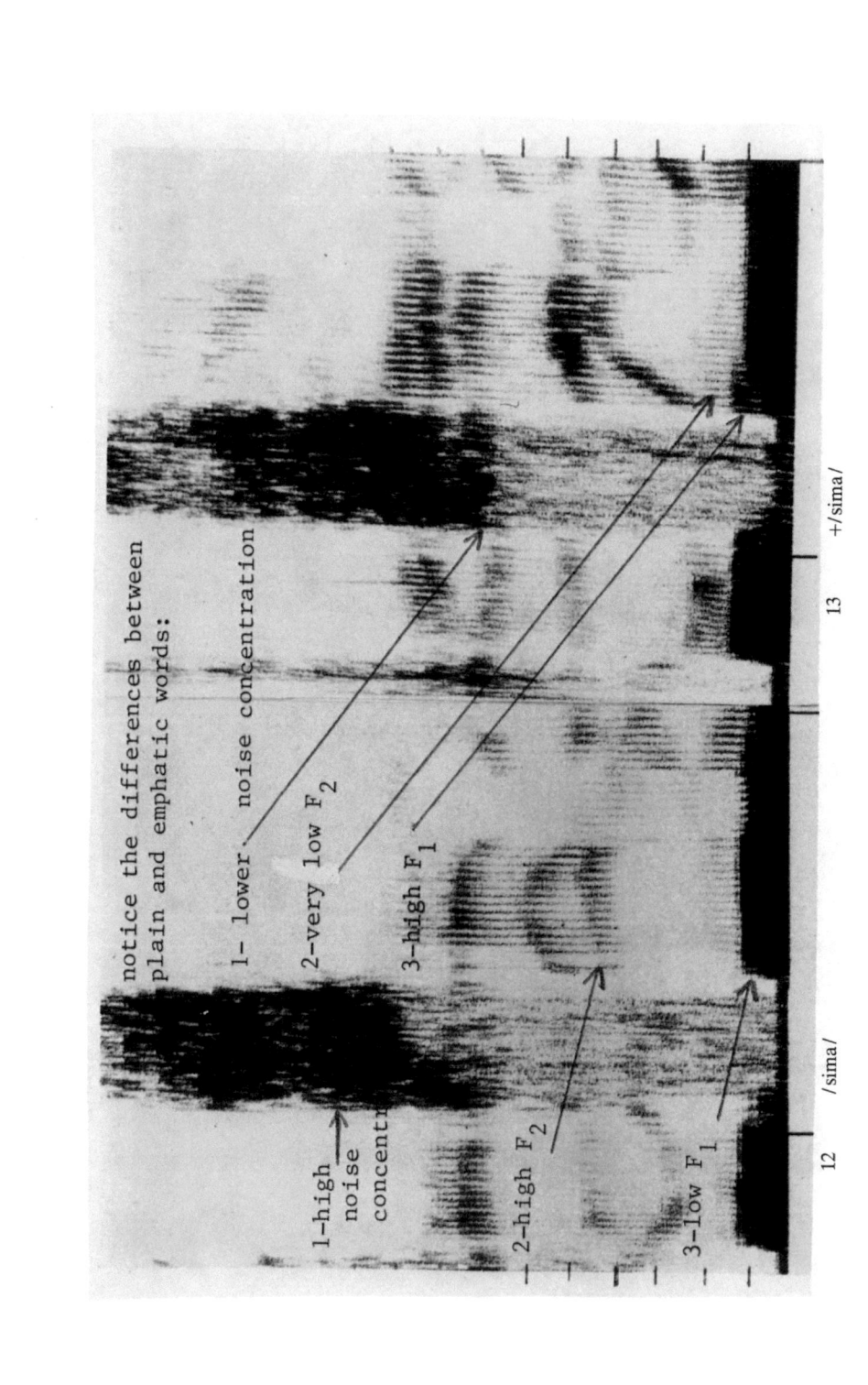

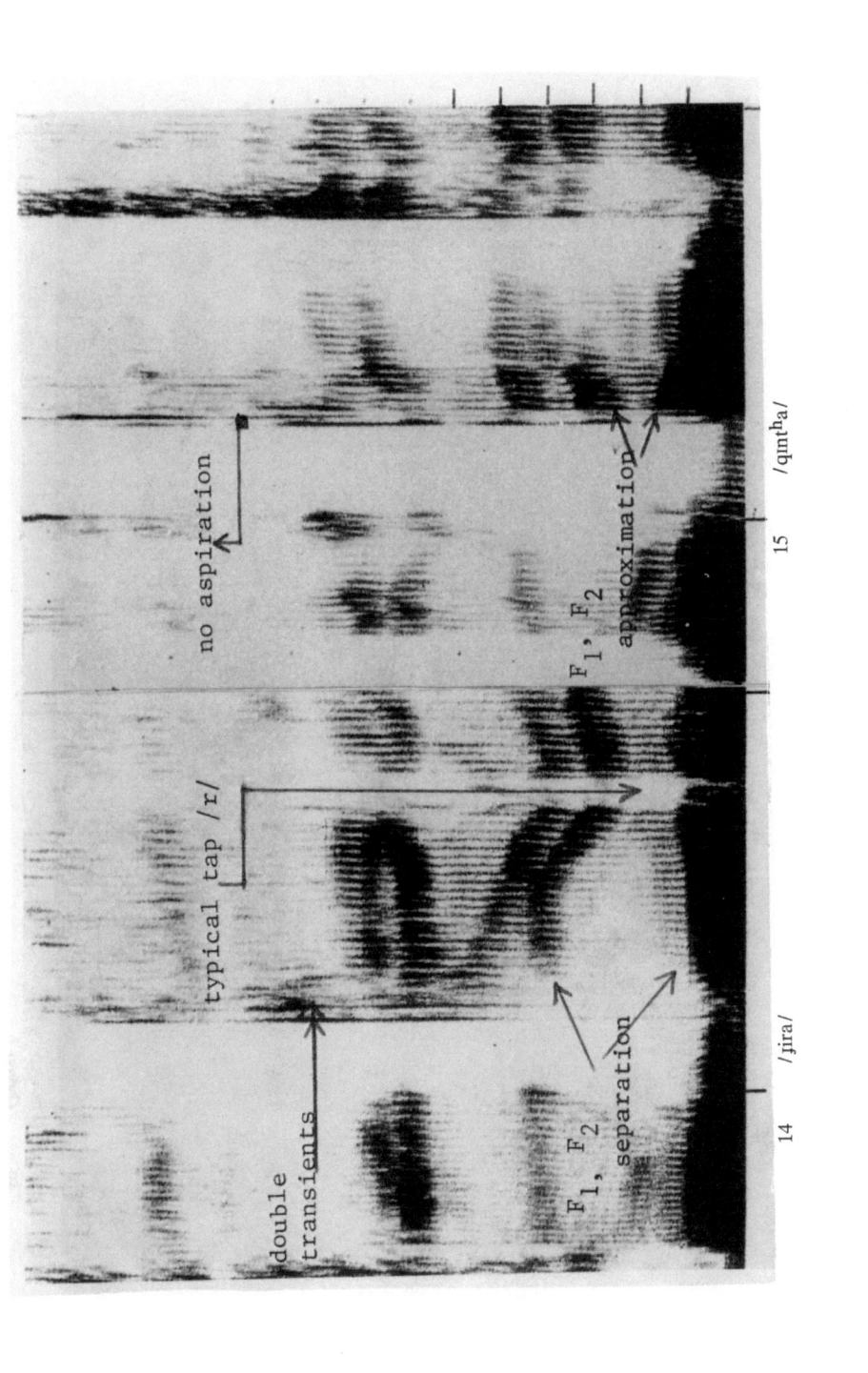

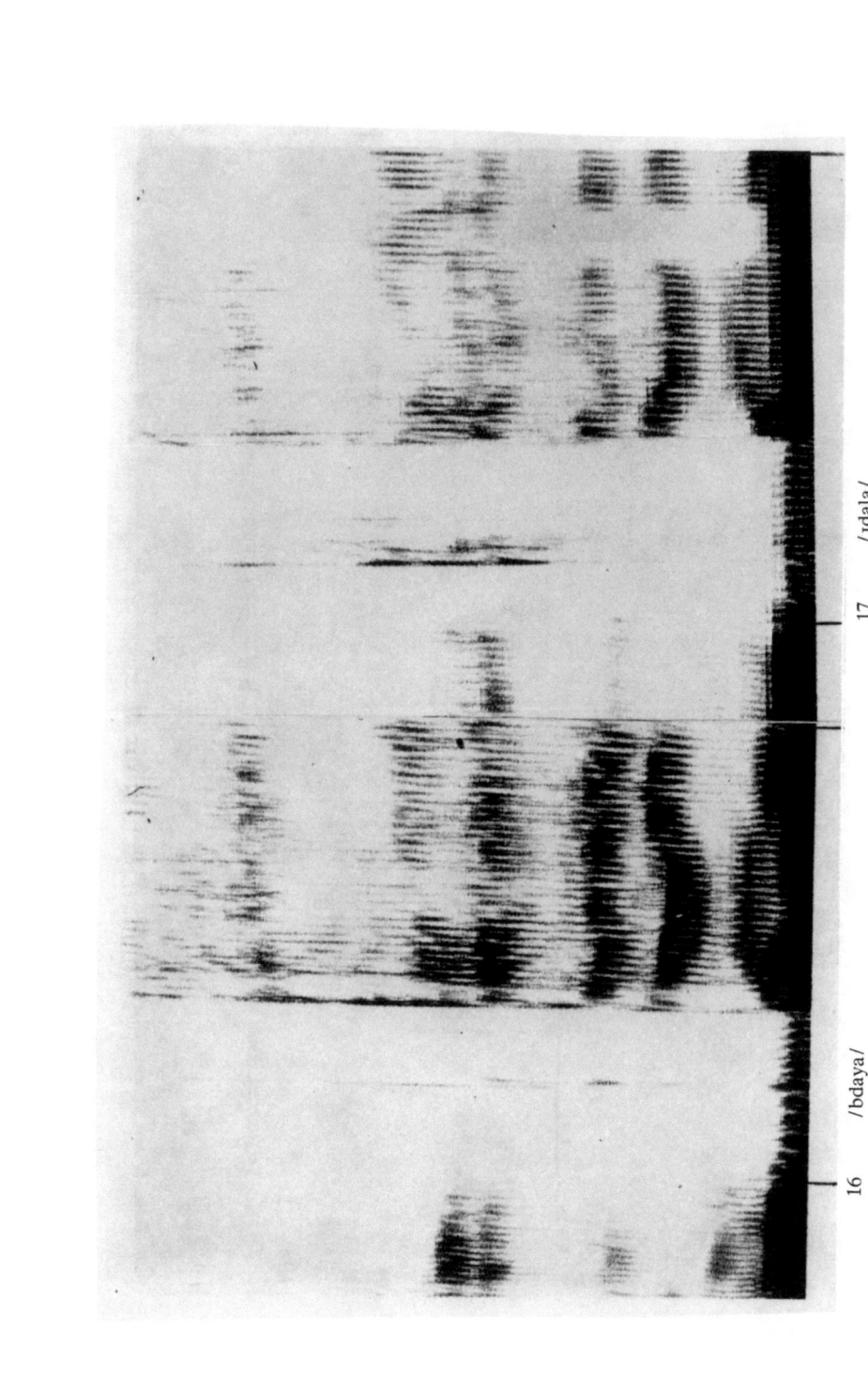

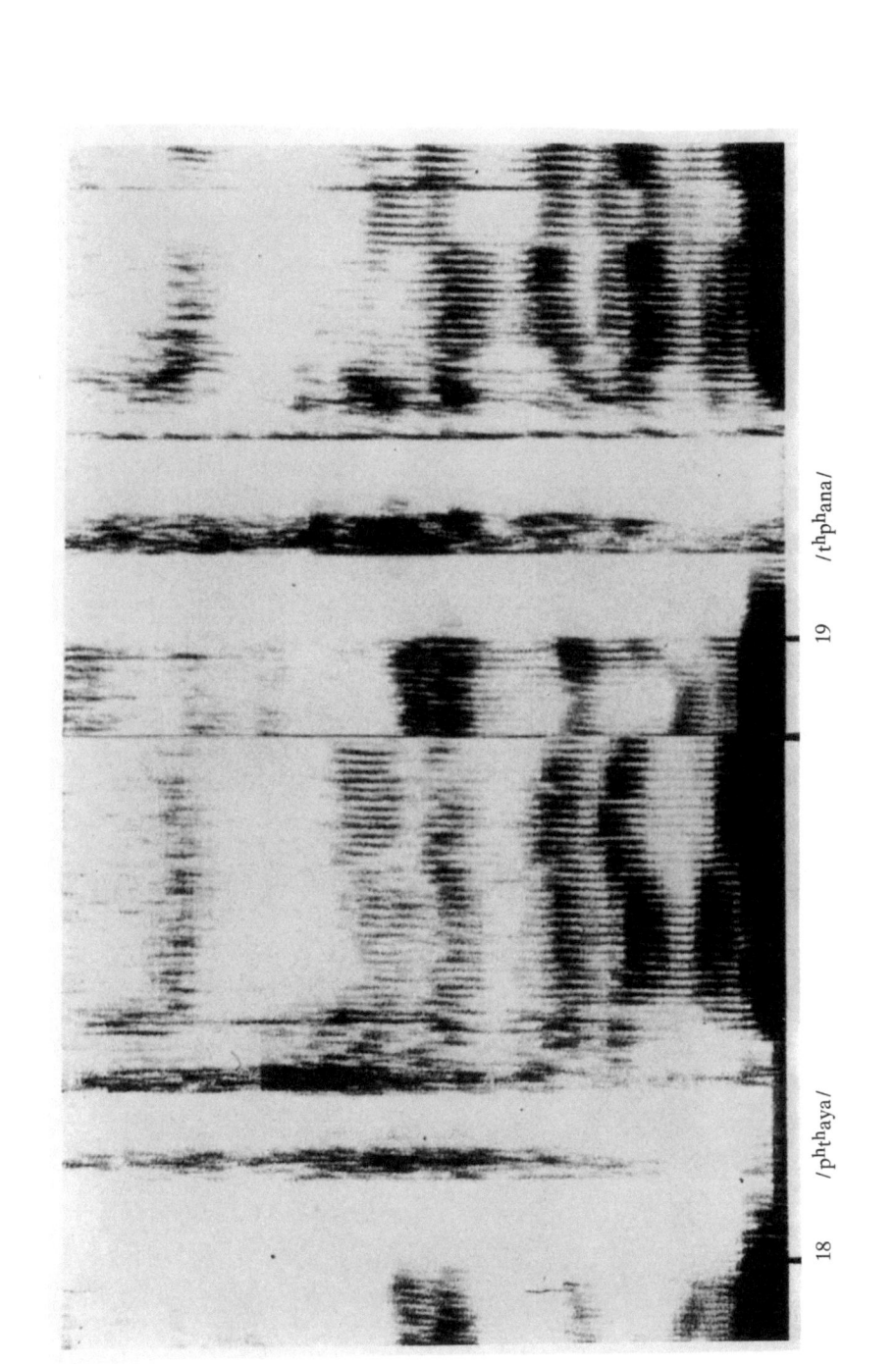

18 /pʰtʰaya/   19 /tʰpʰana/

BIBLIOGRAPHY

Abbeloos, J. B. (ed. tr.) (1890) "Acta Mar Kardaghi." *Analecta Bollandiana.*
Abercrombie, D. (1967) *Elements of General Phonetics.* Chicago: Aldine.
Al-Ani, S. H. (1970) *Arabic Phonology,* The Hague: Mouton.
Ali, L. H., & Daniloff, R. E. (1972). "A Contrastive Cinefluorographic Investigation of the Articulation of Emphatic-Nonemphatic Cognate Consonants." *Studia Linguistica* 26:81–105.
Andrae, W. (1938) *Das wiedererstandene Assur.* Leipzig.
Atiya, Aziz S. (1968) *History of Eastern Christianity.* Notre Dame, Ind.: University of Notre Dame Press.
Badger, G. P. (1852) *The Nestorians and Their Rituals.* London: Joseph Masters.
Bedjan, P. (ed.) (1890–7) *Acta Martyrum et Sanctorum.* Paris.
Blanc, H. (1953) *Studies in North Palestinian Arabic.* Jerusalem: Central Press.
Bosworth, A. B. (1980) *A Historical Commentary on Arrian's History of Alexander.* Vol. 1. Oxford: Clarendon Press.
Britannica/Micropaedia (1985) "Iran." Vol. 21.
Burling, Robbins (1970) *Man's Many Voices.* New York: Holt, Rinehart & Winston.
Catford, J. C. (1977) *Fundamental Problems in Phonetics.* Edinburgh: Edinburgh University Press.
Chomsky, N., & Halle, M. (1968) *The Sound Pattern of English.* New York: Harper & Row.
Colledge, M. A. R. (1967) *The Parthians.* New York: Frederick Praeger.
Cook, J. M. (1983) *The Persian Empire.* New York: Schocken Book.
Cook, J. M. (1985) "The Rise of the Achaemenids and Establishment of Their Empire." *Cambridge History of Iran,* 2:200–91. Cambridge: Cambridge University Press.
Crone, P., & Cook, M. (1977) *Hagarism.* Cambridge: Cambridge University Press.
Cureton, W. (ed. & tr.) (1864) *Ancient Syriac Documents.* (repr. 1967) Amsterdam: Oriental Press.
De Selincourt, A. (tr.) (1954) *Herodotus: The Histories.* Harmondsworth: Penguin.
Diakonoff, I. M. (1985) "Media." *The Cambridge History of Iran,* 2:36–148. Cambridge: Cambridge University Press.
Dinneen, F. P. (1967) *An Introduction to General Linguistics.* New York: Holt, Rinehart & Winston.
Diringer, D. (1968) *The Alphabet: A Key to the History of Mankind.* New York: Funk & Wagnalls.
Durant, W. (1942) *The Story of Civilization: Our Oriental Heritage.* New York: Simon & Schuster.
Encyclopedia Americana (1982) "Adiebene." Vol. 1.
El-Haleese, Y. A. (1971) *A Phonetic and Phonological Study of the Verbal Piece in a Palestinian Dialect of Arabic.* Unpublished Ph.D. thesis. London University.
Emhardt, W. C., & Lamsa, G. (1970) *The Oldest Christian People.* New York: AMS Press.
Fant, G. (1958) "Modern Instruments and Methods for Acoustic Studies." *Proceedings of the 8th International Congress of Linguistics,* Oslo. Pp. 282–362.
Fant, G. (1960) *Acoustic Theory of Speech Production.* The Hague: Mouton.
Fant, G. (1973) *Speech Sounds and Features.* Cambridge: M.I.T. Press.

Firth, J. R. (1957) *Papers in Linguistics 1934–51*. London: Oxford University Press.
Fischer-Jørgensen, E. (1968) "Voicing, Tenseness and Aspiration in Stop Consonants, with Special Reference to Danish." *Annual Report of the Institute of Phonetics–University of Copenhagen*, 3:63–114.
Fox, R. L. (1973) *Alexander the Great*. London: Allen Lane.
Frøkjaer-Jensen, B. (1967) "A Photo-Electric Glottograph." *Annual Report of the Institute of Phonetics–University of Copenhagen*, 2:5–19.
Fromkin, V., & Rodman, R. (1983) *An Introduction to Language*. New York: Holt, Rinehart & Winston.
Fry, D. S. (1968) "Prosodic Phenomena." *Manual of Phonetics* (ed. B. Malmberg). Amsterdam: North-Holland Publishing Co. Pp. 365–410.
Frye, R. N. (1963) *The Heritage of Persia*. Cleveland: World Publishing Co.
Gaber, A. M. (1972) *The Phonology of the Verbal Piece in Cairo Egyptian Arabic*. Unpublished Ph.D. thesis. London University.
Gimson, A. C. (1967) *An Introduction to the Pronunciation of English*. London: Arnold.
Greenfield, J. C. (1985) "Aramaic in the Achaemenian Empire." *The Cambridge History of Iran*, 2:298–313. Cambridge: Cambridge University Press.
Haddad, R. (1970) *Syrian Christians in Muslim Society*. Princeton: Princeton University Press.
Heinrichs, W. (1985) "Written Ṭuroyo." Paper presented at *The 19th Annual Meeting of the Middle East Studies Association*, New Orleans.
Herzfeld, E. (1968) *The Persian Empire*. Wiesbaden: Franz Steiner Verlag.
Hetzron, R. (1969) "The Morphology of the Verb in Modern Syriac." *Journal of the American Oriental Society*, 89:112–127.
Hyman, L. (1975) *Phonology*. New York: Holt, Rinehart & Winston.
Jakobson, R. (1957) "*Mufaxxama* the 'Emphatic' Phonemes of Arabic." *Studies Presented to Joshua Whatmough* (ed. E. Pulgram). The Hague: Mouton. Pp. 105–115.
Joseph, J. (1961) *The Nestorians and Their Muslim Neighbors*. Princeton: Princeton University Press.
Jouguet, P. (1928) *Alexander the Great and the Hellenistic World* (repr. 1978). Chicago: Ares Publishers.
Kim, C. W. (1970) "A Theory of Aspiration." *Phonetica*, 21:107–116.
Klatt, D. H. (1973) "Voice-Onset Time, Frication and Aspiration in Word-Initial Consonant Clusters." *Quarterly Progress Report*, 109:124–136.
Kraeling, E. G. (ed. 1953) *The Brooklyn Museum of Aramaic Papyri* (repr. 1969). The Brooklyn Museum/New Haven: Yale University Press.
Krotkoff, G. (1982) *A Neo-Aramaic Dialect of Kurdistan*. New Haven, Conn.: American Oriental Society.
Ladefoged, P. (1971) *Preliminaries to Linguistic Phonetics*. Chicago: University of Chicago Press.
Ladefoged, P. (1982) *A Course in Phonetics*. New York: Harcourt, Brace, Jovanovich.
Lambert, W. G. (1973) "The Babylonians and Chaldeans." *Peoples of Old Testament Times* (ed. D. J. Wiseman). Oxford: Oxford University Press. Pp. 179–196.
Lehiste, I. (1970) *Suprasegmentals*. Cambridge: M.I.T. Press.
Lehn, W. (1963) "Emphasis in Cairo Arabic." *Language*, 39:29–39.
Maclean, A. J. (1895) *Grammar of the Dialects of Vernacular Syriac* (repr. 1971). Amsterdam: Philo Press.
Maclean, A. J. (1901) *Dictionary of the Dialects of Vernacular Syriac* (repr. 1972). Amsterdam: Philo Press.
Manna, J. E. (1900) *Chaldean-Arabic Dictionary* (repr. 1975). Beirut: Babel Center Publications.

Marogulov, Q. (1935) *Grammar for Adults' Schools*. Moscow.
McCullough, S. (1982) *A Short History of Syriac Christianity to the Rise of Islam*. Chico (Calif.): Scholars Press.
Minifie, F., Hixon, Th. J., & Williams, F. (eds.) (1973) *Normal Aspects of Speech, Hearing and Language*. Englewood Cliffs, N.J.: Prentice Hall.
Mitchell, T. F. (1953) *An Introduction to Egyptian Colloquial Arabic*. London: Oxford University Press.
Mitchell, T. F. (1969) "Review of Abercrombie's *Elements of General Phonetics*." *Journal of Linguistics*, 5:153–164.
Morony, M. G. (1984) *Iraq After the Moslem Conquest*. Princeton: Princeton University Press.
Murray, (1970) "Introduction." *The Oldest Christian People*. Emhardt & Lamsa. New York: AMS Press.
O'Connor, J. D. (1973) *Phonetics*. Harmondsworth: Penguin.
Odisho, E. Y. (1973) *The Role of the Rear Section of the Vocal Tract in Baghdadi Arabic*. Unpublished M. Phil. thesis, Leeds University, England.
Odisho, E. Y., Barber, D., & Scully, C. (1975) "*Tafxim* in Arabic and Neo-Aramaic." Paper presented at *The Eighth International Congress of Phonetic Sciences*, Leeds, England.
Odisho, E. Y. (1975) *The Phonology and Phonetics of Neo-Aramaic as Spoken by the Assyrians in Iraq*. Unpublished Ph.D. thesis, Leeds University, England.
Odisho, E. Y. (1977a) "The Opposition /tš/ vs. /tš^h/ in Neo-Aramaic." *Journal of International Phonetic Association*, 7:79–83.
Odisho, E. Y. (1977b) "Arabic /q/: A Voiceless Unaspirated Uvular Plosive." *Lingua*, 42:343–347.
Odisho, E. Y. (1979a) "Consonant Clusters and Abutting Consonants in English and Arabic: Implications and Applications." *System*, 7:205–210.
Odisho, E. Y. (1979b) "An Emphatic Alveolar Affricate." *Journal of International Phonetic Association*, 9:67–71.
Odisho, E. Y. (1984) "The Neo-Aramaic Dialects: Danger of Extinction." Paper presented at *The 18th Annual Meeting of the Middle East Studies Association*, San Francisco.
Odisho, E. Y. (forthcoming) "A Phonetic and Phonological Description of the Labio-Palatal and Labio-Velar Approximants in Neo-Aramaic." *Neo-Aramaic Studies*. Harvard Semitic Series (ed. Wolfhart Heinrichs).
Olmstead, A. T. E. (1948) *History of the Persian Empire*. Chicago: University of Chicago Press.
Oppenheim, A. L. (1964) *Ancient Mesopotamia*. Chicago: University of Chicago Press.
Oppenheim, A. L. (1967) *Letters from Mesopotamia*. Chicago: University of Chicago Press.
Oraham, A. (1943) *Oraham's Dictionary of the Standardized and Enriched Assyrian and English*. Chicago: Assyrian Press of America.
Osipoff, S. (1913) "Siriaek." *Le Maître Phonétique*, 28:79–80.
Passy, P. (1913) "Langue Excentrique." *Le Maître Phonétique*, 28: 120.
Paulys Realencyclopädie der Classischen Altertumswissenschaft (1893). Wiesbaden: Metzlersche Verlagsbuchhandlung.
Pike, K. L. (1966) *Phonetics*. Ann Arbor: University of Michigan Press.
Polotsky, H. J. (1961) "Studies in Modern Syriac." *Journal of Semitic Studies*, 6:1–31.
Postgate, N. (1977). *The First Empires*. Oxford: Elsevier-Phaidon.
Rassam, H. (repr. 1971) *Assur and the Land of Nimrod*. Westmead: Gregg International Publishers.
Rawlison, G. (1859) *The History of Herodotus*. New York: Appleton & Co.
Robins, R. H. (1970) "Aspects of Prosodic Analysis." *Prosodic Analysis* (ed. F. Palmer). London: Oxford University Press. Pp. 188–200.

Rogers, R. W. (1915) *A History of Babylon and Assyria.* New York: Books for Libraries Press.
Rosenthal, F. (1974) *A Grammar of Biblical Aramaic.* Wiesbaden: Otto Harrossowitz.
Roux, G. (1964) *Ancient Iraq.* Cleveland: World Publishing Co.
Sabar, Y. (1974) "Nursery Rhymes and Baby Words in the Jewish Neo-Aramaic Dialect of Zakho (Iraq). *Journal of the American Oriental Society,* 94:329–336.
Saggs, H. W. F. (1962) *The Greatness That Was Babylon.* New York: Hawthorn Books.
Saggs, H. W. F. (1973) "The Assyrian People." *Peoples of Old Testament Times* (ed. D. J. Wiseman). Oxford: Oxford University Press. Pp. 156–196.
Sapir, E. (1972) "Sound Pattern in Language." *Phonological Theory* (ed. V. Makkai). New York: Holt, Rinehart & Winston. Pp. 13–21.
Scully, C. (1973) "The Problem of Unstressed Vowels and the Coarticulation Within Consonantal Clusters for English." *Journal of the International Phonetic Association,* 3:4–9.
Smith, S. (1926) "Notes on the Assyrian Tree." *Bulletin of the School of Oriental and African Studies.* Pp. 69–76.
Smith, S. (1960) "Ashurbanipal and the Fall of Assyria." *The Cambridge Ancient History,* 3:113–131. Cambridge: Cambridge University Press.
Stevens, K. N. (1971) "Airflow and Turbulence Noise for Fricative and Stop Consonants: Static Considerations." *The Journal of the Acoustical Society of America,* 50:1180–1192.
Strevens, P. (1967) "Spectra of Fricative Noise in Human Speech." *Readings in Acoustic phonetics* (ed. I. Lehiste). Cambridge: M.I.T. Press. Pp. 202–219.
Toynbee, A. J. (1947) *A Study of History* (abr. D. C. Somervell). New York: Oxford University Press.
Tsereteli, K. G. (1978) *The Modern Assyrian Language.* Moscow: NAUKA Publishing House.
Vööbus, A. (1951) *Studies in the History of the Gospel Text in Syriac.* Louvain: CSCO.
Waterfield, R. E. (1973) *Christians in Persia.* New York: Barnes & Noble.
Watt, W. M. (1974) *The Majesty That Was Islam.* New York: Praeger Publishers.
Wright, W. (1890) *Lectures on the Comparative Grammar of the Semitic Languages.* Cambridge: At the University Press.